The
Triangle
Formula
of
Success

EXCELLENCE KNOWLEDGE

△

VISION

Dedication

This book is a tribute to the Ms. Johnson's of the world,
great teachers who inspire students to achieve purposeful
greatness and excellence through a love of learning,
in and out of the classroom called *Life*.

∧ **Acknowledgements**

I first want to thank God for the opportunities He has blessed me to experience, which have shaped and molded me into a better human being.

I also recognize the following people for contributing to this endeavor:

My wife, Monya, for her unwavering support and devotion to my mission;

My loving mother for allowing her "baby" to see the other world beyond the Sullivant Gardens Housing Projects;

My family, friends, and even total strangers who have been instrumental in assisting me on my journey;

My wonderful editor, Chiquita Mullins Lee, for her tireless efforts;

My talented book designer and project coordinator, Terry D. Anderson;

And last but not least, you the reader.

From the bottom of my heart, I thank you all.

Table of Contents

△ **Preface**

Some people see life as a series of pictures. Others feel it as increments of time. Some take to life according to how they see the glass —either half-empty or half-full.

I see life in terms of mathematical formulas. This is probably a unique perspective. People define math as complex and inaccessible. Algebra, trigonometry, geometry, and calculus challenge those with math anxiety. But like anything else in life, math is as simple as you make it. It needn't be complicated at all.

Remember grade school math? It was simple. Reliable. Concrete. One pencil plus one pencil equals two pencils. Four pencils minus one pencil equal three pencils. Position each pencil so that their ends touch and you create a triangle. And they tell me that the triangle is one of the strongest configurations on earth.

My triangle formula for success consists of three equal sides, and each side is as powerful as the next. In the upcoming pages, I'll discuss the three sides of this powerful triangle and reveal how vision, knowledge, and excellence create the formula for a successful life.

"The right angle for approaching a difficult problem is the 'try-angle.'"

—Unknown

I developed a love for math in the second grade. Addition (+). Subtraction (−). Simple multiplication and division (x and ÷). Inequalities and comparisons (< and > and ≠). My teacher was Ms. Johnson. She was a sweet lady who enjoyed helping her students reach their full potential. I'll never forget her. She was a light-skinned woman, about 5-feet-8. She wore glasses with big lenses and metal frames, compatible with the style of the late 1970's and early 1980's. She even wore her hair in a feathery Jheri curl. She had the perfect demeanor for dealing with kids. She was patient and calm and I loved being in her class.

She made me want to do well, and I did. When I entered the third grade, after a year of Ms. Johnson's guidance, math became more than just a subject.

One day, at the start of the school year, I saw Ms. Johnson in the hallway.

"Lawrence, how are you doing?" she asked with a warm smile.

"I'm doing fine," I said.

"Are you still doing well in math?" she asked.

I smiled and nodded.

"Well, I've got an assignment for you. I'm teaching a whole new set of kids now. How would you like to come to my room and grade my students' quizzes and math tests?"

I was surprised by her question and didn't answer right away.

She continued, "But only after finishing your in-class assignments, and of course you'll be able to look at the answer key. Would you like to do that?"

I smiled again and said, "Yes, ma'am."

I was so excited. Whenever she needed me, I was right there grading papers. The thought of being Ms. Johnson's designated math grader consumed me. Several times a week, I would find myself asking her if she had any math grading for me to do.

"Not today, Lawrence, but I'll let you know when I do," she replied.

For those brief few moments on quiz and test-grading day, I was someone special. So special, in fact, that my peers looked up to me. I even sat at a desk right next to Ms. Johnson's. It was a privilege to be her assistant.

"There is a mathematical explanation for everything."

Λ
—SQuire Rushnell

The answer key gave me insight into another world of math: the perfect formula for success. Add a little here. Subtract a little there. I saw how math problems were calculated—the entire process—from a new perspective. Each addition and subtraction step I observed brought joy to my heart that to this day, I still can't fully explain.

Ms. Johnson saw something in me that even I didn't know was there. Who would expect a third grader to identify his own hidden purpose-driven talents? Ms. Johnson, however, would watch me as though she knew, even back then, that math would play a vital role in my life.

When the school year was almost over, I got an even bigger surprise. Not only had I had the privilege of serving as Ms. Johnson's assistant, but there was also a bonus. I would be getting paid for my efforts! I was a nine-year old math entrepreneur. Ms. Johnson rewarded me with a shiny $.50 cent piece, which I spent immediately. Boy was I ecstatic! I know. I know. That isn't a lot of money by today's standards, but the takeaway experience would prove invaluable a few months later.

Little did I know that in the summer of that same year I would come face-to-face with a simple mathematical formula that could change every aspect of my life forever. The challenging part of the mathematical formula to lasting success? Calculating what it would require of me if I diligently followed it. Thank God I was committed, and still am to this day!

While reading The Triangle Formula, you'll laugh. You'll cry. You'll be inspired. And you'll want to inspire others by helping them achieve a life of greatness. More than 25 years later, The Triangle Formula is still producing amazing results in my life. And it will in yours, too! Let's begin . . .

Chapter One

△ *My Roots – Beating the Odds*

I grew up in the Sullivant Gardens Housing Projects in Columbus, Ohio. Reared in a single-parent household on welfare for 18 years, by all accounts my future looked bleak. My neighborhood was typical of many inner-city poverty stricken communities in America. I'll never forget the littered landscape, the stench of garbage, the shattered liquor bottles. I often had to sweep the basketball court in front of my apartment before I could work on my jump shot.

These things I dealt with without a father. I saw the man who supplied half my DNA about three times, all before age ten. He never read me a book, or came to watch me play sports, or attended a single parent-teacher conference, or called me one time just to say hello. Most damaging, he never once said to me, "I love you, son." And each time he showed up—a rare occasion indeed—he was drunk. This was his way of coping with the burden of his responsibility. Me. He never gave me the satisfaction of seeing him sober during his brief visits. My father gave me exactly what he knew how to give me. Very little. And growing up without him was devastating.

"I had to teach myself how to be a man."

—Tupac Shakur

△

He passed away at 40 of liver damage. I was 16 years old. I didn't bother to attend his funeral. I did not know the man, only his name. I don't even have a photograph of my father. And no matter how hard I try, I can't get a clear picture of him in my mind. The pain of abandonment lingers, but I have since forgiven him.

There was an irony about living in Sullivant Gardens. Most of the streets were named after former U.S. presidents, including Van Buren (first name, Martin), McKinley (first name, William), Pierce (first name, Franklin), Coolidge (first name, Calvin), and Buchanan (first name, James), which was my street. There were, however, no presidents of countries living in my neighborhood. No doctors or lawyers, either. And very few intact families with a mother and a father in a stable household.

> ### *"The absence of structure in the life*
> ### *of a child is the absence of love."*
>
> —Edward F. Sommer

Δ

Perhaps this is why I could not watch an entire episode of The Cosby Show in the 1980's. At that time, Bill Cosby's message didn't fully resonate with me. He was a doctor, and his wife Claire, an attorney. The rest of the Huxtable household? Well, they were emotionally balanced children who seemed not to have a care in the world.

My experience with the "real world" was quite different from that of Cosby and his television family. In fact, I was in denial about his revolutionary outlook for African Americans and other minority groups who dared step outside suffocating stereotypes. Was it really possible to attain the success of Dr. Cliff Huxtable? I was somewhat skeptical. In those days, I didn't see examples of such success in my neighborhood.

Sullivant Gardens was shut down in the late 1990's. Still, I can remember how I felt about living there. I was so ashamed and humiliated to live in that environment that I even made some tiny adjustments. When I began to receive heightened notoriety as a consensus top five high school basketball prospect on the national level, I purposely would leave off the apartment number (#C) when giving my address to a college coach or out-of-town friend that I'd met at camp. I didn't want them to know that I lived in the projects. And whenever someone from a nicer part of town would give me a ride home, I often hinted when getting off the West Mound Street exit that I lived on the other side of I-70 West where the houses were. Sometimes, I would have them drop me off there. The majority of the white families who inhabited these houses were just as poor, but at least, I rationalized, they lived in a house.

Humiliation feels the same whether you're poor, at an unhealthy weight or in a rocky marriage, or buried under a mountain of debt. Four entirely different circumstances. But there is a solution for living your dreams. For every humiliating circumstance, I apply the same formula. No magic. No gimmicks. Just principled-living with a purpose.

"Where you are right now doesn't necessarily mean you will stay there."

Λ   —James Redd

Horrifying criminal violent acts were regular occurrences in Sullivant Gardens. From drug transactions and gang-banging to knockouts, live, up-close, and in-person, we saw it all. Because of all the action, a former schoolmate at Wehrle High School jokingly nicknamed my housing projects Madison Square Gardens, after the famed, legendary event venue in New York City. Word on the street was that even the police feared patrolling our neighborhood because of its reputation and standing.

I witnessed many traumatic experiences, but one violent incident in particular had a lasting impact on me at the tender age of nine. Across the field, about 100 yards from my apartment, was a softball/baseball diamond. It was rarely used, except when neighborhood kids played the "dare" game and climbed up and over the backstop and down the other side. One summer day, a softball game was played there. A part of me wishes it had never been played.

Our neighborhood team was pitted against a visiting recreation center from the Westside. We were all black. Their team was all white. After all these years, I still don't know why they agreed to play the Sullivant Gardens Recreation Center team on our own turf, especially when racial tensions were still relatively high in the early 1980's.

I don't recall our coach's name, face, or motives, but he was forced to use players who were too old and had no association with the team up to that point. On this day, they decided to suit up. Anyone who dared stop them risked a severe beat-down of the worst kind. Our poor coach had no choice but to let these hooligans play against kids who were several years younger than they. (I was too young to be a part of this team, comprising teenagers between the ages of 14 through 16. My reference to "our" team referred the neighborhood in general.)

Before the game started, the white team was already terrified by the site of their unusual surroundings! The "new" players were smacking pitches over the fence for homeruns on just about every plate appearance.

They taunted the other team throughout the game. Inning after inning, the score became more and more lopsided. Finally, the game was called. Thank God. What happened next, though, scarred me for the rest of my life. But it was also my life-transforming, eureka moment that sparked a desire to achieve a life of greatness.

After getting beat by double digit runs, the distraught white team walked off the diamond with their heads hanging low. Soon, they were startled to find out that a humiliating loss just wasn't enough.

From beatings with softball gloves, to sucker punches, hand slaps, and foot-stompings, all manner of violence was inflicted on the teenagers for no apparent reason than the color of their skin. They would not be leaving Sullivant Gardens without a beat-down. All of them, including their muscular coach. No one was spared this savage attack. With the little energy they had left, they ran to their vehicles parked on the periphery of Sullivant Gardens. Most outsiders dared not park or set foot within the confines of our 'hood for fear of reprisal.

The white coach was the last to leave after staying behind to make peace. He tried everything to calm the instigators. I can still see the fear on his face. I can still see his hands open, his arms extended, as he tried to reason with them to stop their onslaught. Unfortunately, his efforts didn't work.

This coach had a weightlifter's physique and obviously worked out on a regular basis. But no amount of weightlifting could prepare him for what came next.

One resident watching the game from the sidelines took the liberty of joining the beat-down action. He grabbed an aluminum softball bat and swung it as hard as he could and hit the coach on the side of his head at his temple. I distinctly remember the incident as if it were in slow motion. The shock of a horrific event seems to make time stand still.

Stumbling to his car in a daze, the coach, along with his team, finally exited Sullivant Gardens. To this day, I cannot believe that blow to the head didn't kill him. Strangely, he was thought to be the villain, but without just cause. And the perpetrator? He was considered a hero, righting decades of economical, social, physical, and emotional abuse on innocent blacks by "the man" and his kinsmen. This is what that whack to the temple symbolized to those supporting this cowardly act.

Young observers that day saw that act of violence as an entirely acceptable way to vent internal anger. How quickly the words of Martin Luther King, Jr.—that violence never works to right any verifiable wrongs—were forgotten.

To say I was shocked would be an understatement. I ran non-stop back to my apartment, slammed the front door behind me and hurried to my bedroom. Out of breath, I sobbed uncontrollably for several minutes, recounting what I had just witnessed. Senseless violence can do this to a fragile young mind and spirit.

You may be wondering what this gut-wrenching story has to do with The Triangle Formula of lasting success—vision, knowledge, and excellence. Everything! The horrific display of violence changed the course of my life, forever. That day, at the tender age of nine, I had an epiphany: if I were going to escape the harsh world of ghetto life, I would need to learn a systematic formula that left little room for constant errors. I knew right then that the life I dreamed about would eventually manifest itself one day if . . .

"There must be a vision of something bigger than today."

——Jesse Duplantis

Λ

My vision of a better tomorrow involved a passion for knowledge and an unwavering commitment to excellence, to do the right thing regardless of the obstacles in front of me. This is the abbreviated formula for lasting success and each component has a related factor such as faith, wisdom, and the ability to overcome adversity. You'll read about all these factors in the upcoming pages.

Your reason for obtaining a life of excellence may be altogether different from mine. Whatever your reason, this simple approach will help you in your journey. And always remember that success is a journey, not a resting place!

This tried and tested formula—vision, knowledge, and excellence—works. In coming pages you'll learn the keys to sustained success for individuals and organizations alike that hold dear to these principles. Some of the individuals are household names, while others are not. Each of them had to make a commitment to vision, knowledge, and excellence, often working long days and nights. Have you ever had to work long into the night just to finish a project? Sometimes, long nights result from stress, worry, heartaches, and struggles. Other times, you just want to make it to the next level. The upcoming chapters will address these issues. But before we go on, there is something about you that I want to ask, "What's keeping you up late at night?"

for Discussion

1. Name three challenges that you have already overcome.

2. Write down three of the biggest challenges in your life today.

3. Write down three steps you can take to start overcoming your challenges.

_____

_____

_____

_____

_____

_____

_____

_____

_____

_____

_____

_____

_____

_____

_____

_____

_____

_____

Chapter Two

△ *What's Keeping You Up Late at Night?*

No, I'm not talking about heartburn from gulping down your food right before bedtime after a long day at work, although the wrong foods can wreak havoc on a stressed-out body! What I'm referring to is a burning desire to attain an elusive goal that dominates your every waking thought, all day and all night. A great antidote for insomnia and stress is The Triangle Formula of Success. When you incorporate The Triangle Formula of vision, knowledge, and excellence into your daily life, you'll be amazed how easy it is to get a peaceful night's rest!!

The Triangle Formula has been a big part of my life since I was a little boy, though at 6'9, most people can't imagine me ever being little! Of course, as a Christian, I would be remiss if I didn't acknowledge the source of my talents, abilities, and financial resources—God Almighty.

After that fateful day on the softball diamond, God began to uncover the hidden talents and abilities that had always been there, waiting to be revealed along with my specific assignment in life. Those qualities would have never surfaced unless I believed that tomorrow would be better than today. I had to really believe, and then take determined action. The same holds true for you on your journey.

"If you keep your eyes on the promise you'll withstand the process."

—Les Bowling

△
___

Had I not made a conscious effort to move in a positive direction, I would have become a product of my environment and manifested a self-fulfilling prophecy.

I'm grateful to have lived in an environment of lack, despair, and disarray. I appreciate the lessons I learned from The Triangle Formula and how it has become an integral part of every area of my life. As I'll share in a later chapter, I paid a heavy price when I failed to recognize that success isn't a resting place; it is a journey. In my arrogance I thought that I'd arrived. Huge mistake.

Great organizations and successful individuals understand that their best is good, but there is always room for improvement. Since the universe is still expanding, can't I reasonably conclude that I too have only scratched the surface in maximizing my talents, abilities, and resources? In your journey of success, you must also answer this question in the affirmative—"Yes!!"

"Don't be discouraged; everyone who got where he is, started where he was."

—Unknown

So, back to my earlier question. What's keeping you up at night? Are you worried about your finances? Your health? Your business? Your marriage? Your children? Polls show that Americans are most concerned about wealth and health, in that order. Regardless of the current obstacle, you can achieve success physically, relationally, financially, and spiritually. Are you ready for your breakthrough? Are you ready to put your mind at rest? Well, keep reading. Below are some specific steps to take.

First, see yourself or your company arriving at an intended destination. This is **vision**. In order to reach the goal you envisioned you must concentrate on the smaller steps, momentarily stopping for a fill-up and to rest-up, while keeping the larger vision in mind.

Here's another suggestion—unless you have a photographic memory, write down your vision. After you have written your vision, regularly check the progress of each stated goal. Celebrate each goal along the way, remembering that a life of greatness or a thriving business never rests on previous accomplishments.

Second, increase your knowledge base. **Knowledge** is useless, however, unless you absorb and apply it. And when you apply knowledge, you develop wisdom: knowing what to do, then doing what you know.

The third principle determines whether people and organizations will achieve sustained success. The greatest basketball player of all-time woke me up again to this truth when I was a wet-behind-the-ears rookie in the NBA. It was an experience that reaffirmed The Triangle Formula's most unforgiving rule: we must keep moving forward. Keep learning. Keep achieving. When we don't, lasting success will eventually pass us by, waiting to reward the next person in line regardless of ethnicity, gender, or origin of birth. My mentor-in-passing moment with Michael Jordan dealt with the spirit of excellence, which I cover in greater detail in Chapter Seven. In short, this commitment to **excellence** is the cornerstone of The Triangle Formula.

"Success is never final."

—Winston Churchill

Λ

Okay, I admit to having two things that sometimes keep me up late at night. They are servant leadership and the creation of additional income streams.

Servant leadership is about creating value in the life of others. For me, it starts with my wife and children. As a husband, I want to serve and love my wife, Monya, for the express purpose of strengthening our lifelong, committed relationship. The way I serve my wife will largely determine what type of man my daughter, Nyah, gravitates to and marries when she is of age. Quite frankly, this responsibility is a bit intimidating since I never had a father to emulate. But I certainly relish the opportunity.

When it comes to my son, Lawrence Elijah, the way I treat his mother and sister will shape his behavior toward women. Again, this task can be daunting since my father never showed me how a good man treats a woman. I mention my father's lack of modeling and support for illustrative purposes, only. A parent is the greatest teacher in these and other areas, but no excuse is acceptable if I fail to deliver on my promise.

The Triangle Formula—vision, knowledge, and excellence—has a proven track record. Obstacles and setbacks come to test our character, but staying on course ensures a successful outcome.

In the area of servant leadership, I have yet another priority—the **Lawrence Funderburke Youth Organization** (LFYO), which creates programs for young people, and the audiences I address on behalf of LFYO. I can empathize with the pain and hurts of young people because, for the most part, I've walked in their shoes. But the new millennium brings an entirely different set of challenges than those I experienced as a child back in the 1980's, and even the 1990's. Unfortunately, hopelessness in inner-city communities seems to have kept pace with rapid advances in technology. Violent acts committed by young people have steadily increased. Children are dying in our streets every day. Across the nation, an alarming number of youth are dropping out of high school. Their anger and rage will be heard loud and clear one way or another. As a servant leader, my responsibility is to decide how to address it. In Chapter Nine, I discuss The Triangle Formula approach to helping at-risk youth obtain a promising future.

"Hopelessness is a family destroyer and soul killer."

—Rick Johnson

Δ

After creating value and servant leadership, I am committed to developing income streams. My income streams to date have included:

1. Professional sports
2. Writing and publishing
3. Public speaking
4. Sound financial investments

For some people, the creation of multiple income streams comes naturally. For others, the difficulty lies in recognizing the value of your precious resources and maximizing those with the greatest potential. And for a number of people, having too many options can be paralyzing, depleting their energy, and clouding their focus. With so many options to choose from, what some of these people choose to do is nothing. Instead of growing their own opportunities, their hard-earned dollars go into someone else's pocket, or they earn very little interest on bank accounts that barely keep pace with inflation. Rather than be complacent, these people need to learn about the benefits of creating value.

As a friend and financial guide once told me, "Creating value for others generates income. People don't mind paying for a service or product when they know and feel they are getting their money's worth." Value creation is other-focused rather than self-focused, and this is the key to building the life we aspire to live.

If you're a budding entrepreneur, you need to know the key to developing a profitable business. That key is creating value. Ask yourself this question, "What thing of substantive value—the thing that will improve customer's lives—do I bring to the marketplace?" Only you know the answer to this question, and the answer or answers will determine your bottom line. All of us have multiple talents and resources that we can maximize. You can start by identifying the strongest of these talents and then developing them to the extent that they provide valuable services to others and become income streams for you. Notice how each of these factors—servant leadership, and developing income streams—both add value and depend on others for success.

Your monetary assets warrant consideration, but other assets are important, as well. Before concentrating on financial net worth, I'd like to make one suggestion: an entrepreneur or new hire college graduate should make it a priority to analyze his/her personal net worth. Be honest. Assess your personal strengths (assets) and weaknesses (liabilities). If you need help, ask family members and close friends what they think are your obvious strengths and weaknesses. But don't be surprised by the answers if they're brutally honest.

"Never have a conflict between your purpose and your goals."

—Tony Dungy

Λ

You can boost your personal and financial net worth by increasing your assets as your liabilities remain unchanged. You can likewise reduce your liabilities, which will increase your asset base. A third scenario —increasing your assets while simultaneously reducing your liabilities —is the most ideal for building net worth.

We've got to know who we are, or else we'll never experience a fulfilled life. You've heard the adage money doesn't make a person. You can believe it. You'll never find true contentment in material riches. Through many painful lessons and horror stories, I've learned the truth of that adage.

"Many a man has found the acquisition of wealth only a change, not an end, of miseries."

—Lucius Annaeus Seneca

Λ

As I've said before, I love mathematical formulas. Here is a useful formula for assessing your net worth:

Good -   Assets (strengths/positive attributes) ↑
             — Liabilities (weaknesses/unfavorable attributes)
             = ↑ Net Worth

Better - Assets (strengths/positive attributes)
             — Liabilities (weaknesses/unfavorable attributes) ↓
             = ↑ Net Worth

Best -   Assets (strengths/positive attributes) ↑
             — Liabilities (weaknesses/unfavorable attributes) ↓
             = ↑ Net Worth

For example, a personal net worth profile might look something like this:

Assets —	Liabilities =	Net Worth
team player, personable, compassionate, critical thinking skills, handles criticism well, etc.	procrastinator, passive, poor eating habits, educational background	more assets boost net worth

This assessment tool takes just a few minutes, but can make a world of difference in your life and the lives of others. Don't get discouraged if your personal net worth is in the red. Be committed to improving your liabilities to reflect a positive net worth. Your situation will improve in time if you don't give up. On the other hand, if you sport a favorable net worth, please keep adding to it. Always remember the golden rule of The Triangle Formula: don't get too comfortable with your level of success, because an unforeseen fall might be imminent!!

What's Your Pull?

You can learn a lot from observing group dynamics. Like-minded individuals tend to congregate together. Positive thinkers attract positive thinkers. Negative behaviors attract negative behaviors. Unethical business practices attract unethical business practices. It is true that objects of mass tend to gravitate to one another! You can learn something about yourself by observing the kind of things that pull at you.

Another beneficial tool highlights two factors that influence us: protective factors and risk factors. These factors can hinder our success and keep us awake at night or they can enhance our success, give us peace, and reinforce our self-worth. Being keenly aware of both is absolutely critical, because whatever we gravitate to speaks volumes about the quality of life we desire for ourselves, as well as for our children and grandchildren!

Harvey Halliburton, a criminal justice expert and youth social worker with the Franklin County Juvenile Courts in Columbus, Ohio, brought these factors to my attention. These factors are generally used as a tool for assessing at-risk youth, as I once was. In fact, I have outlined my factors in the section below. Anyone can identify their own protective factors and risk factors. Note that protective factors are individual- or company-specific. Risk factors can be general and/or individual-specific.

Below are the factors that influenced me when I was a child:

Protective Factors	Risk Factors
sports, education, passion for learning, coaches/mentors, self motivated, job opportunities, loving mother	neighborhood, poverty, peer pressure, single-parent home, naysayers, gangs, availability of drugs

Protective factors and risk factors can also apply to people facing all kinds of challenges. A dieter might identify these factors:

Protective Factors	Risk Factors
friends, weight watch support groups, positive attitude, vision (here's the new me!!)	fast-food restaurants, time management, depression, upbringing, prior eating habits, commercial ads

Someone seeking financial freedom might name these factors:

Protective Factors	Risk Factors
income stream opportunities, charitable giving, available mentors, support from friends, ready to change bad spending habits	one income, debt, availability of easy credit, lack of current financial knowledge, family history in this area, Keepin' up with the Joneses

An entrepreneur might note these factors:

Protective Factors	Risk Factors
Competitive advantage, customer service, results-oriented approach, organizational culture	barriers to entry, competition, market share, outdated operational methods, changing marketplace

We can gravitate to one set of factors or the other. Our protective factors positively motivate us to achieve the life we dream of. At the opposite end of the spectrum, our risk factors unfortunately cause us to short-circuit the beautiful life that is ours to live. When I was a young boy the gravitational pull to my protective factors, in effect, shielded me from falling victim to my risk factors.

Think of it in terms of accounting. Every time we gravitate to a protective factor, our success account receives a credit. But when we succumb to a risk factor, our success account receives a debit. At the end of the day, we tabulate our accounts to determine our profit-and-loss position. Simple enough, right?

Whatever your protective factors are, identify and hold dear to them. These factors create value in your life, prepare you for service, and stimulate self-worth. Energized by these positive qualities, you'll start to discover new ideas for income streams. All the components work together and maximize the effectiveness of The Triangle Formula. Eventually, you'll experience the life you dream to live! Ready?

for Discussion

1. Write down three talents or resources that could be offered as a service for others and as a potential income stream for yourself.

2. Write down three risk factors and protective factors.

3. Name three negative behaviors that keep you from attaining your vision; now think of ways to counteract them.

_____

_____

_____

_____

_____

_____

_____

_____

_____

_____

_____

_____

_____

_____

Chapter Three

△ *The Vision of the Heart*

While in middle school I met Doug Lessells at Cooper Stadium. Doug was a sports reporter for WCMH-TV NBC 4. I'd watched him on television and was excited to meet someone famous. That evening, I walked up to him, shook his hand, and introduced myself. What came out of my mouth surprised him, leaving an indelible mark that he would never forget. I said matter-of-factly, "Mr. Lessells, my name is Lawrence Funderburke. You don't know who I am yet, but you will one day." Eight years later as a sophomore at Ohio State in the second round of the NCAA tournament in Lexington, Kentucky, I was interviewed by none other than Doug Lessells. During the interview, he told a listening audience via satellite what I said back then to him at Cooper Stadium. Coincidence or destiny?

> *"The further a person can look into the future, the greater the chances of success in life."*
>
> △ —Robert Kiyosaki

Amazing when you stay focused on a goal regardless of the obstacle, the law of averages will often bend in your favor. Go on. Let your vision be heard. Don't be afraid to back it up! That's why the first side of the Triangle Formula of Success is vision. You must have vision and be willing to work toward that vision.

It was my willingness to work that gave me a chance to meet people such as Doug Lessells. As a young man, regardless of the season, I worked. In the fall I sold hotdogs and cokes at Ohio Stadium, home to the OSU Buckeyes football team. In the winter months I shoveled snow off the sidewalks and driveways of a nearby trailer park. In the spring and summer I was a vendor at Cooper Stadium, home of the Columbus Clippers.

(The Columbus Clippers were the AAA-affiliate of the New York Yankees for almost three decades. For the 2007 and 2008 season they partnered with the Major League Washington Nationals.)

These jobs taught me that work offered monetary awards, but it also allowed me to meet people from all walks of life, who would influence the course of my journey.

As a child my vision was to escape the harsh world of the ghetto. The right way! No drug selling. No illegal hustling. Education and the value of hard work were, and still are, the driving forces behind my vision.

I loved school. Competing in the classroom was something that I looked forward to each day. Keep in mind that back then, and it is still unfortunately the case today, the value of education isn't respected by some people in the 'hood. They will label you a sellout if you are passionate about education. If you're black, the terms, "nerd" and "white wannabe" are commonly used as descriptions.

I've never understood how being educated poses a threat to people who live in the 'hood. I'm fortunate that I didn't buy into that trap. If you're a young person and you've heard similar outlooks from people in your neighborhood, please don't let them distract you from your goals. I know this sounds strange, but you should welcome the detractors. This proves that your vision for a life of greatness is valid. For this very reason, The Triangle Formula was written especially for you. You do have a destiny to fulfill. Don't let anyone stop you!

My mom used to call me Huckleberry Finn, after the character from Mark Twain's famous novel. I was always on the go, determined to lead a life of greatness in spite of my environment. Like young Huckleberry Finn, I had a lot of lessons to learn on my journey. One of those lessons was to consistently work hard in spite of the obstacles in front of me.

A great many people in this country have a survival-of-the-fittest outlook on life. Subsequently, they never bother to maximize their talents, abilities, and resources. They accept defeat in the face of the frustrations of their current situation. Tragically, this mindset is passed on to their kids and grandchildren, who also succumb to the same debilitating thinking —that a prosperous life of maximized potential is only for a select few, those rare individuals born into a life of privilege.

I can argue that impoverished communities offer few opportunities for economic empowerment. I speak from experience. But once I stepped outside the comfort zone of my boundaries—my housing projects —an oasis of economic possibilities did, in fact, exist. And more were at my disposal! However, I could find them only through the vision within my heart.

My physical eyes saw lack and scarcity. But there was a visionary inside me, and with these "eyes" I saw boundless opportunities full of promise. This is what visionaries call thinking or seeing outside the box. The road less traveled is available to everyone, but few choose to walk down it. Why? Because it is off the beaten path. It is foreign to people who are complacent because they prefer to stay within their comfort zones. These people choose to travel the familiar road.

"The future belongs to those who see possibilities before they become obvious."

—John Sculley

Λ

In hindsight, every job that I had during my formative years did much to prepare me for a much larger vision. My initial vision was to work and earn a few bucks. That early vision ultimately opened the door to a vision with greater responsibility and exponentially higher rewards —becoming a big-time college athlete and NBA player. Peter Gabriel's 1980's hit "Big Time" was one of my favorite songs that inspired me even back then. But first I had to pass the test, appreciating and being grateful for the lessons I learned from my smaller vision. Fortunately, a vision can start small and gain size and power.

Your vision is probably quite different than mine, but the process to achieve a life of greatness is the same—The Triangle Formula. Have a vision, gain knowledge, and perform with excellence.

In the book, *The Principles and Power of Vision*, Dr. Myles Munroe discusses how to identify vision and bring it to pass. He maintains that sight and vision are not the same. Repeat, sight and vision are not the same. As a matter of fact, they often contradict one another. Dr. Munroe writes, "Sight is the ability to see things as they are; vision is the capacity to see things as they could be."[1] The two keys to fulfilling vision are:

1) Clearly identify your stated goal (or purpose).
2) Avoid procrastination. Get moving.

Our lives are full of ways to exercise these principles. For example, one of the greatest joys women are blessed to experience is bringing a precious life into this world. But the extra weight that accumulates during the process is an unwelcome byproduct. My wife, Monya, has given birth to two beautiful children, Nyah Ariel and Lawrence Elijah. Taking these principles into consideration, Monya explains how she was able to maintain a healthy weight during pregnancy, which made it easier to shed the unwanted pounds after giving birth to our son:

> "I first had to incorporate good eating habits, to counteract the cravings for certain unhealthy foods. It is important to prepare your mind for healthy eating—for you and the baby. Instead of eating big portions three meals a day, I ate four to five meals a day and smaller portions, usually every two or three hours. This approach boosts metabolism, which is instrumental to shedding extra weight. Next, I concentrated on building muscle through weight training. Cardio sessions were also important in loosing the extra weight."

With our daughter Nyah, Monya recalls that she did not have healthy eating habits. She remembers how her body looked after giving birth. Not as tone as she would have liked. Monya said it took her about two years to get back to working out. "Once I started my routine, I had to work hard to return to my pre-pregnancy fitness level," she stated. That mental image compelled her to implement some changes while pregnant with Elijah.

The vision she maintained with our son strengthened her commitment and she made every activity measure up. Her eating habits. Exercise programs. Cardio sessions. Within five months, Monya lost over twenty pounds without traumatizing her body, and she accomplished this through the power of vision. Eight months later she reached her goal, losing an astonishing thirty pounds!

Maybe you're not the physical fitness type. But if you're ready to take your body to the next level, Monya's advice will help:

> "Find a picture of someone that you like—their body type—that is realistic for your physique and lifestyle. You might also try locating an old picture of yourself when you were happy with your body, your confidence, and your appearance. Hang it up somewhere so that you see it on a daily basis. Always remember that everything starts in the mind."

Monya stated that she is inspired by one of her personal trainers, whose physique and dedication to physical fitness she admires. "Every time I leave from training with her, I notice that I really focus on my diet and cardio routine. Because I know that I can look like that." (Be sure to consult your physician before beginning an exercise program. For more information on reaching your ideal weight, go to www.thetriangle-formula.com.)

You must visually see what you want your body to look like. Although the challenge is great, keep moving toward your vision!

Finding Your Passion

For some people, passion is a buzzword. It doesn't conjure up excitement. It's just a word. Nothing more. Perhaps you've never thought much about uncovering something radically exhilarating and life-transforming. But inside every human being dwells a passion to accomplish the extraordinary. This section will help you unlock that hidden treasure. Webster's dictionary defines passion as "an outburst of strong feeling." But the best way to understand passion is to view the lives of uncomplicated, extraordinary men and women who exude this quality throughout every fiber of their being. Think Oprah Winfrey. Think Tiger Woods. Think Akrit Jaswal.

Oprah regularly tells her audience, "When you follow your passion, great things will follow." I agree. I asked my wife to describe Oprah's passion. Monya remarked, with one sentence. Simple. Definitive. "She is driven to make the world a better place by educating the general public on inspirational topics, and through compassionate philanthropy."

*"Only passions, great passions,
can elevate the soul
to great things."*

—Denis Diderot

Λ

Tiger's golf prowess has been well-documented over the years. A prodigy since his toddler years, he is dedicated to winning every tournament that he enters, often bringing out the best in the competition. Tiger's laser-like focus is legendary. He was born to be a professional golfer!

Akrit Jaswal is a medical genius who lives in India. At the age of seven—that's right, seven!—he performed his first surgery. Now in his teens, he told the viewing audience on The Oprah Winfrey Show that he wants to become a doctor so that he can take away pain in the lives of others.[2] He also wants to be the first person to find a cure for cancer. Soon! And he may very well be the first.

In layman's terms, your passion is doing something that you would gladly do for free everyday if all of your basic needs were met. No one has to beg you. No motivational pep talk.

Oftentimes, a life of purpose is found in a life of passion. You pursue your passion simply because it is an honor to complete the assignment for which you were called.

But when we aren't passionate about our life's purpose or vision, our true talents and abilities will forever be hidden from a world that desperately needs them. Here are a few tips to help you cultivate vision for your life of greatness:

1) Have you ever experienced a dream that was surreal, taking you to the precipice of a life of greatness? What were the hidden gems in the dream? What lessons did you learn?

2) Think back. Okay, way back. Close your eyes and let your heart gravitate to that goal or dream waiting to be fulfilled.

3) When in doubt, ask a loved one or friend to tell you what they feel you are most passionate about. Sometimes, those closest to us can see the obvious in our lives, even when we are unaware of it.

Now, take that first step of faith.

for Discussion

1. Why is it important to have a vision?

2. Why is it important to write down your vision?

3. Write down three things that you are passionate about achieving.

Chapter Four

△ F.A.I.T.H. – For All Individuals There's Hope

Sometimes, our journey of faith leads us through unexpected detours. My own faith journey led me overseas and then to California. After graduating from Ohio State in 1994, I was drafted by the Sacramento Kings. I didn't play for Sacramento at that time, however, and chose to play overseas for three years. I played for Sacramento from 1997 until 2004, but I missed the entire 2003-2004 season while recovering from a partially torn Achilles tendon. Some people doubted I would ever play again. I heard comments such as, "He's getting old" and "He's made his money and probably doesn't have it in him to compete at that high a level again after going through a difficult surgery." But I kept the faith that one day I would step on an NBA court so my daughter could see me play in person for the first time. By the grace of God, I did. The Chicago Bulls signed me late in the 2004-2005 season. After my stint with the Bulls, I returned to live in Columbus.

We have examined the first side of the triangle and learned about the power of vision. Now, let's look at the connection between vision and faith. The connection is actually pretty simple. Faith helps you to actualize your vision.

On my journey, I've met people who understand the connection between vision and faith. Here is a quote from one of them.

> "Faith is the very thing that activates and moves us. When we set a goal, we strive to obtain it. But without faith, the goal can never be achieved. Either you have it or you don't. The way you find faith? Find your purpose in life first."

These are the words of Rydell Gibson. Rydell is founder of T.R.I.P.O.G., (Thoughtful Reverence-Inspired People Of God), a placement facility for displaced boys, ages 7 to 19, in Sacramento, California. Some of the boys have been abused, both sexually and physically, at a young age. Many others have become wards of the state after being abandoned and neglected by their parents or legal guardians.

While living in Sacramento, I met Rydell. We were at a men's Bible study group one evening and he shared with me his passion to help these boys deal with and overcome life's many challenges. I stood amazed, listening to this laid-back, well-dressed native of Cleveland, Ohio, who, with his muscular build and wavy-hair bears a striking resemblance to singer Keith Washington. Whenever Rydell discusses the inhumane treatment that these boys have experienced, his compassion comes through, and tears often well up in his eyes. In addition to his generous nature, he is big on friends and family. He enjoys holidays, cooking, and is a magnetic combination of qualities that make him jovial, confident, low-key, and real cool. Rydell is the perfect mentor. Even today, he remains as passionate as ever about T.R.I.P.O.G., and the boys who have become part of his extended family.

Rydell and I view life through different sides of the same prism. While I approach life in terms of mathematical formulas, Rydell creates acronyms for challenges and solutions. I can't visualize what he sees unless he explains it to me, and through his use of acronyms, his explanations become clear. This is his gifting. When I called Rydell and mentioned that his F.A.I.T.H. acronym would be the title of my fourth chapter, he immediately came up with another one for the very same word. "Finding another instrument that helps." So true in term's of our life's journey.

Rydell explained how he instills, or enhances the faith of the boys in his group homes, given that they have low self-esteem as a result of past traumas or positive toxicology screen.

"I let them know that I understand their feelings. Their reality! Encouragement and support are also critical. Helping them gain minor successes likewise strengthens their level of faith. Or it could be as simple as telling them, 'I am going to be a big brother to you.' Or, 'I am going to take you to a sporting event.' Showing an interest in their well-being helps, especially when they've been abandoned by the very people who brought them into this world. Subsequently, they see something in you that they never before have seen in any individual they've come into contact with during their brief lives."

Rydell added, "There are people who've never been told, 'You're beautiful. You're smart. You're intelligent. You've got a good head on your shoulders. You can achieve success.' Sometimes we think only material things or personal accomplishments make a difference. In fact, our words have power to increase another's faith." It can be as simple as saying, "I love you."

Walking Alone

Faith is never more tested than when we walk alone on our journey. After I committed to living by The Triangle Formula, I assumed all of my friends would follow me. I was sadly mistaken. Very few of my peers wanted to walk that road with me.

Most of my neighborhood friends didn't understand my commitment to education and work at an early age. On one of my report cards in middle school, I received a "C." Distraught, I stared at the card on the bus ride home after school.

A classmate asked, "What's wrong?"

"I got a 'C' in one of my classes," I answered solemnly.

"You trippin'," he shot back. "A 'C' is pretty good."

Then he let the other students on the bus know about my "silly disappointment."

On another occasion, some of the kids from the neighborhood came to Cooper Stadium to pass time. Lord knows I tried, but there were moments when I could not avoid running in to them.

One of them said to me, "Look at Lawrence, working hard to make a couple of dollars."

Rarely did I miss a day at work when I was a young teenager. Yet, on some occasions, I paused to consider their point of view.

"Maybe they're right, that school ain't cool. And what's the purpose in working to earn a few dollars right now?"

> *"Faith is believing*
> *in things when*
> *common sense*
> *tells you not to."*
>
> —George Seaton

Λ

But somehow, I kept the faith that my efforts would produce untold benefits down the road. I had reservations about going forward and leaving my peers behind, but faith kept me focused on my long-term vision.

Eyes Off The Prize

She started off with a bang! This time her weight loss program would succeed. Nancy Fryar (not her real name), a retired, fifty-something grandmother lost six pounds in the first month. Her goal: lose 30 pounds in six months. Nancy used the assessment we described in Chapter Two and gravitated to her protective factors. She was eating healthy, drinking plenty of good water, and exercising regularly. Then she veered off the path. She took her eyes off the prize. Fear is usually the culprit. She reflected:

"Once I got motivated it was easy to stay on my routine. But something always comes up to get me off of it. I was really doing well. I hadn't felt this hopeful in a long time. Suddenly, everything just seemed to fall apart. As a result, I got depressed. Everyday I'd look into the mirror and cry, 'I need to do something about my weight.' But I just couldn't get back to the level of success I once enjoyed."

Do you share a similar story? You get off to a good start. But, out of nowhere, a distraction interrupts your journey. Then another problem surfaces and compounds the situation further. Frustration sets in and the goal is aborted. Inside you scream, "How did this happen?"

Let's take a close look into Nancy's mindset. She admitted, "Something always comes up to get me off of [my routine]." In other words, she anticipated that a problem would eventually appear—her greatest risk factor. And guess what? Like clockwork it did, right along with several of its friends.

"Talk unbelief, and you will have unbelief;
talk faith, and you will have faith.
According to the seed sown will
be the harvest."

Λ ———Plato

The opposite of faith is fear, and fear was the thing Nancy dreaded the most. Her obstacles weren't contrived. They were real.

During difficult times, faith doesn't minimize the obstacles that come our way. These character tests are a part of life. Keep this in mind

—the way we see life's challenges determines how effectively we deal with and overcome them. It is the vision of the heart that must be magnified. Not our problems. We control the lens that minimizes our fears and maximizes our faith. The opposite is true also. This is the law of cause-and-effect.

Faith draws us to our protective factors. Nancy's many protective factors included regular exercise; good eating habits; proper hydration; compliments from family, friends, and even total strangers; and her own personal vision—"Get ready for the new me!" Nancy's risk factors included past relationships, lack of focus and, of course, fear.

Faith and fear exist throughout our journey. But they can never peacefully co-exist. We can never be full of faith and full of fear at the same time. One is fed while the other starved. Doubts inevitably come before, during, or after we start our journey toward a life of greatness. We might even second-guess ourselves but, regardless of doubt, we take the next step. Fear, on the other hand, paralyzes us. We want to move forward and take that next step, but we can't. Understanding the difference between doubt and fear is vital to achieving your goal. Please don't confuse the two.

> ### *"Life is a wilderness of twists and turns where faith is your only compass."*
>
> —Paul Santaguida

Λ

We've got to wake up each day and tell ourselves, "Today will bring me closer to my dream." Our lives will change for the better once this habit becomes a part of our daily routine.

Nancy shared with me that the difficult part now is getting motivated again. She knows that she can. "But I have to get my mental outlook together first." She also admitted to cheating on her diet while getting comfortable with the fast results, and blaming the lack of progress on a faulty scale and an unforgiving mirror.

Before she retired from her job, Nancy never had a weight problem. When she was working, she was always active. After retiring, she had more time on her hands and she slowly began to gain weight. Nancy explained, "Every time I walk in the kitchen I stop at the refrigerator or browse through the cupboards."

Like so many retirees approaching their golden years, Nancy admits to falling victim to a common mindset: "What's the point in staying physically fit at my age?" She discusses the root cause of her struggle:

> "One of the things I need to do is work on my inner self. Right now, I don't feel I'm pretty on the inside. I really don't know who I am. Once I can start to love me, things will get better. Then again, I feel that I don't want it badly enough because I'm not doing anything about it."

Chapter Two advises us to take inventory of our personal net worth (assets or strengths – liabilities or weaknesses = personal net worth). This inventory impacts our level of faith. When we don't know who we are, life will always be a struggle.

"Prepare to have your hope restored that you have a unique destiny waiting to be fulfilled."

Λ   —T.D. Jakes

Sometimes our identity gets lost inside another person. Monya, my wife noted, "A lot of people live their lives through someone else. When the relationship is over, their lives begin to crumble. Because they put so much energy into that other person, they lose themselves, and they don't know who they are anymore." Find yourself. Find faith. Find a life of greatness.

"C'mon, You Can Do It!"

When our son was six months old, I would often hold his hands and help him take a few steps. Perhaps more than anything, my encouragement and faith motivated him to take those steps.

"C'mon, you can do it!" I'd say.

His eyes got big. Those wobbly legs would not be denied. The more I encouraged him, the more confident he got with each step. Eli's exuberance was evident. The sounds of joy. The facial expression of anticipation.

Those five words gave him the determination he needed to take that first step. Then the next. Then another.

Now I say to you, "C'mon, you can do it!"

Faith will compel us to get moving to achieve the life we dream to live. Martin Luther King Jr. once said that faith is taking the first step when we can't see the whole staircase. Don't let fear and unbelief stop you in your tracks. You've got a destiny to fulfill!

Without faith, your vision will never get off the ground. Do you see yourself becoming a better parent? You need faith. Reaching your ideal weight? You need faith. Starting your own business? You need faith. Getting out of debt? You need faith.

Again, faith does not attempt to minimize the obstacles in front of you. This is merely wishful thinking. Faith magnifies the vision within your heart. The vision cannot be denied. It will not be stopped. Your vision will be fulfilled. Why? Because faith is your guiding compass when you cannot see the first step…or even the next step. Don't worry about the outcome. Vision keeps you moving forward; and faith's got your back!

for Discussion

1. Why is it important to have faith?

2. What is the connection between faith and vision?

3. Write down three times in your life when you
   benefited from standing alone?

_____

_____

_____

_____

_____

_____

_____

_____

_____

_____

_____

_____

_____

_____

_____

_____

_____

_____

Chapter Five

Addicted to Knowledge

Reading has been a passion of mine since I can remember. In elementary school I heard that we humans use only 10 percent of our brains. This statement motivated me to fill up the remaining 90 percent! Not sure how true this is, but I do know that we are so wonderfully made that our capacity for knowledge is practically endless.

To the chagrin of my wife, the side of our bed that I sleep on looks as if two librarians got in a knock-down, drag-out fight. (I know. I know. This is diametrically opposed to their nature.) Books are scattered everywhere—a couple of Bibles, roughly 20 investment or finance periodicals, and volumes on topics ranging from parenting to public speaking —so much so that a fleet-footed ballerina dancer would be hard pressed to nimble through the maze without a fall. The knowledge from these resources is priceless. Knowledge can be leveraged infinitely more than money, which is obviously a limited resource for most of us.

Our schools of higher learning attract multinational organizations eager to land the best and brightest minds. These corporations offer new graduates compensation packages that would strike envy in the CEO of a small company. Why do the graduates receive such substantial offers? Because they have acquired knowledge. Knowledge alone can separate an average employee from a superior one; a marginal company from an industry leader; and an average team from the game's best.

"Some students drink at the fountain of knowledge —others just gargle."

—Unknown

One summer, I attended an executive education program at Stanford University as part of the National Basketball Players Association continuing education program. During evening breakout sessions, current and former NBA players were paired with relatively young graduate students to review daily readings and class lectures. Every player was in awe of the students' zeal for knowledge. Most of the graduate students had already mapped out a blueprint for their entrepreneurial endeavors in Silicon Valley!

A passion for knowledge and education is contagious, and it is to our children's benefit that this passion is contagious. Pastor Zachery Tims once said, "You have to model your commitment to education in front of your children." My daughter, Nyah, has internalized my habit (good and bad) of sifting through dozens of books next to her bed. A war zone? Yes. A fertile ground for learning? Indeed. She will grow up knowing that a woman's success is limited by the lack of knowledge she possesses, and not because of gender or the color of her skin. Knowledge makes the difference! I've asked our daughter on several occasions what she wants to be when she grows up. Her response? A teacher! I should have known.

Scouting Your Success

Most fans who watch professional or even college sports are not privy to the arduous scouting process that occurs between each team. Professional teams use scouts and video coordinators to study opposing teams' and individual players' strengths and weaknesses.

The NBA pre-game scouting report is exhaustive. On a board made of several dividers approximately 10 to 12 feet wide, five feet high, and some four feet off the floor, coaches "school" their players on the nuances of the opposing team, including various offensive and defensive strategies, each player's go-to moves and deficiencies, scoring averages, rebounds, block shots, assist-to-turnover ratios, etc. And depending on the team's routine (before or after the scouting report), several minutes of highlights from their opponent's past games are shown on television monitors right above the board. This process is repeated at every game regardless the number of times a team has played an opponent during the season. During the playoffs, a two-inch binder and several video tapes are given to each player to study his opponent, collectively and individually. Counting pre-season, regular season, and playoffs, a team could conceivably play the same opponent up to 12 times! (And you probably thought players spent just enough time to suit up in the locker room and then run around playing tag-you're-it for a couple of hours.)

"Make preparations in advance. You never have trouble if you are prepared for it."

—Theodore Roosevelt

Λ

Similarly, you have to scout your life of success. You must perform the necessary due diligence to become the parent you were called to be. The employee or business owner you were called to be. As you scout for information in different areas of your life, you will understand how to be wealthy, healthy, and whole.

Everyone can benefit from scouting in the area of finances. Find ways to reduce your debt while scrutinizing every financial outlay. Try tracking your expenditures, according to type and cost, in a financial journal everyday for three months. You'll be shocked by the results. My wife and I initially did this several years ago and we almost fainted. And by all accounts we are not spendthrifts! This three-month analysis is the first step to financial freedom because it forces you to set-up a realistic budget.

"Handle your personal finances as if they were going to be printed somewhere for everybody to see."

—Ron Blue

Λ

For an in-depth analysis of your spending habits, track monetary outlays for six months or up to a year to account for seasonal expenditures, such as back-to-school clothes, vacations, utility fluctuations, etc. You can also find information on the website to assist you in this area.

If you want to achieve a healthy lifestyle, you can easily acquire knowledge about good thinking habits, exercise, and nutrition. Below are some healthful suggestions. Adhere to a diet of 4-5 meals throughout the day, consisting of lean meats, fish rich in omega 3's, whole grains, nuts and legumes, fruits and vegetables, dairy products (in moderation), protein shakes and nutritious snacks, and good water, and the goal will be yours for the taking. Generally, you should be eating smaller portioned meals every 2-3 hours. And go organic if your budget can afford it! (Please visit www.thetriangleformula.com for additional insights on achieving a healthy lifestyle.)

"Our health is our most valuable asset."

Δ —Dr. Ted Broer

As discussed in Chapter Two, knowing who you are and what you were placed on this earth to offer the world—your positive net worth guided by a sense of purpose—are the keys to being whole and at peace. Believe me, I have tried to find fulfillment outside of this formula and it did nothing but leave me more frustrated and incomplete.

Take a proactive approach to scouting your life of success. You will never regret it! See where you want to go, have faith that you'll get there, and incorporate the knowledge to make it happen.

An Unlikely Mentor

Don't underestimate the value of books, periodicals, and yes, even commercials. Their wisdom presents mentor-in-passing moments that can truly be life-transforming. How often have we been inspired by something we have read or heard? You could probably recall dozens of these moments.

Former all-pro running back with the New York Giants, Tiki Barber, was featured in an SUV commercial for a leading automaker in his last season. Most people who watched paid little attention to what he said at the end of the commercial. Why? The SUV was black, had shiny chrome rims, and stood out in the hustle-and-bustle of the New York City skyline. The vehicle made the statement, which is what a product/service is supposed to do in a 30 second (or shorter) commercial.

If I'd ask seven people who repeatedly saw the commercial what they remembered most about it, they'd probably say:

"The car in general."
"The chrome rims."
"The New York scenery."

"The color of the car."
"The brand of the car."
"Nothing in particular."
"The athlete."

The athlete might be the last thing they remember about the SUV commercial, but Tiki Barber can share the road to success. Reflecting on his journey to becoming one of the NFL's most efficient running backs of all-time, Tiki shared a secret that separates a life of greatness from a life of mediocrity. The secret is not complicated. Ready? He said, "Opportunities are seldom perfect. But I've learned that if you're not ready for them, they may not come again." Whenever I am the keynote speaker at an event, I ask audience members to repeat Tiki Barber's epic words.

"The sure way to miss success is to miss the opportunity."

 —Victor Charles

Opportunities must be recognized. We must be aware of them when they come!

Although his athletic ability had not yet been exhausted, Tiki retired from the game to take advantage of the seemingly unlimited opportunities outside of football, notably broadcasting. He decided it was time to walk away on his own terms. Of course, sports fans questioned the sanity of this unusual decision. But timing is everything to the holder of destiny!

Hindsight Is 20/20

Some of our best sources of knowledge are other living and breathing men and women. We call them mentors and they are worth their weight in gold.

You've heard the expression, "Hindsight is 20/20." That's what a mentor has—perfect hindsight. A mentor provides foreknowledge to help mentees minimize the effects of life's pitfalls and maximize life's opportunities. Whatever I've needed mentoring in—spiritual matters, parenting, marriage, leadership, health and nutrition, or business and personal finance—someone has either stepped forward, or I've sought out the necessary mentor to assist me in my journey. I believe quality mentors come along for a special assignment to help their mentees maximize God-given talents, abilities, and resources.

I have a high tolerance for pain, but I don't like to feel it. Instead of experiencing the anguish that comes through trial-and-error, I tend to gravitate to people who possess 20/20 vision in areas where I need guidance. Humility is a pre-requisite here since reaching out to a mentor shows vulnerability!

In key areas, some of my mentors include:

Charity Mentor - Lloyd Harvego, owner of the five-star Firehouse Restaurant in Sacramento, opened his heart, arms, and wallet to children in my non-profit organization when I was playing for the Kings. He hosted disadvantaged youth at the Firehouse for a lesson in fine-dining etiquette at no charge, and invited them to his suite to watch the AAA Sacramento River Cats play a baseball game. I can't thank him enough for his contributions to LFYO in making dreams come true for area youth.

Spiritual Mentor - Dan Springmeyer has been a spiritual father figure to me for almost a decade. When we met, I was a wet-behind-the-ears rookie in the NBA. He helped prepare me to deal with the temptations that accompany NBA life, and taught me what it truly means to be a caring husband.

Parenting and Marriage Mentor - Gus Parker, a successful doctor, has shown me what it means to be a great father and husband. A very humble man, he raised three children who grew into emotionally balanced adults. Each of them aspires to become a doctor, too. I've also gleaned much from his commitment and dedication to the sanctity of his marriage to his lovely wife, Cheryl.

Real Estate Investment Mentor - Bob "Skip" Weiler has taught me how to analyze real estate deals, including cap rates, triple-net leases, growth and location factors, and contingency protective measures. As president of one of central Ohio's most successful real estate development and brokerage firms, he is as compassionate about philanthropy as he is about business, which he learned from his father.

Shareholder Value Mentor - Steven A. Davis, CEO of Bob Evans restaurants, discussed with me what it takes to succeed as an African American in the corporate world. His response, "It's about one word, and it doesn't have a thing to do with color—produce. Results are what matters to shareholders!"

Leadership Mentor - Former New York City mayor, Rudy Giuliani, has been a true mentor-in-passing. He is one of the most down to earth celebrities I've ever met. One summer, during a rendezvous with

Rudy over lunch at the prestigious New Albany Country Club, he covered his leadership style (and empowerment options for the poor, which I'll discuss in Chapter Nine.) He told me, "Leadership is never more tested than during times of crisis." His interest in the hurts and pains of other people helped revitalize the American spirit during one of our country's darkest days to date—9/11.

The tuition-free education I received from these individuals will last a lifetime. The words of 19th century sentimental poet and educator, Henry Wadsworth Longfellow, still ring true today: "A single conversation across the table with a wise man [or woman] is better than ten years' study of books."

"If you find tall grass, you can usually find a path that someone has walked."

—Ronnie Chan

Λ

(In Chapter Seven, I discuss the straightforward mentoring advice in the area of excellence from basketball legend, Michael "Air" Jordan.)

"So You Want To Be A Billionaire, Huh?"

Nearly every teenager knows who the wealthiest person on the planet is—Bill Gates, of Microsoft fame.

But do you know what NBA basketball star LeBron James and Warren Buffett have in common? If you guessed lots of money, you're correct. But were you aware that King James has bowed down to the world's second richest man to pay homage and glean from his vast wealth of knowledge?

If you regularly watch MTV, BET, or ESPN, you might not be familiar with Warren Buffett. Here's a small hint: He owns GEICO Insurance, you know, those hilarious caveman commercials!

LeBron James has sought the investment and business guru to learn more about the otherworldly game he dominates. A billionaire many times over, Warren Buffett has agreed to share (surprisingly) his wisdom with LeBron and his management team. Warren Buffett even flew up from

Omaha, Nebraska, in his private jet to watch LeBron and his Cleveland Cavaliers play the Denver Nuggets on March 25, 2007!

LeBron aspires to become a billionaire one day. He couldn't have picked a better mentor than Warren Buffett and his company's stock to accomplish this goal. Warren Buffett is CEO of Berkshire Hathaway. You might want to grab a glass of water for what I'm about to share next. Get this, as of March 2007 one Class A share of his company's stock cost almost $110,000. No, this isn't a misprint. But if you'd bought the stock in the early 1990's when it was around $7,000 a share, it would have grown to well over 1,000 percent!

Choose your mentors carefully. Their value is priceless.

The Knowledge Gap

Someone once said, "Know your limits, but don't limit your knowledge." Today, the gap between the haves and the have-nots isn't necessarily about color or some other antiquated factor; it's about knowledge. Those who leverage knowledge successfully are rewarded handsomely. Period.

Granted, we cannot deny the economic gulf that exists not only in America, but around the world as well. The tragedy of Hurricane Katrina highlighted the growing economic disparity in this country between poor or middle class New Orleanians and persons of privilege. It was horrific to see people left behind who lacked the resources even to leave the city when the storm hit. This disparity has to change!

When we preach economic scarcity as the gospel, we inhibit the growth of knowledge in disadvantaged communities and countries. The result? A self-fulfilling prophecy.

"We tend to become what's expected of us."

—Michelle Morton

Λ

Hurricane Katrina should wake up our country to the reality that every child deserves a quality education regardless of color or economic standing. Knowledgeable mentors must also step forward and walk each child through the process of success. Let me repeat, walk each child through the process of success. And it is a process. Likewise, people in disenfranchised communities need access to financial literacy and new business start-up loans with favorable interest rates. These are the avenues through which the cycle of poverty can and will be broken. Teach. Show. Empower.

The Triangle Formula of Success cannot be achieved without knowledge. Fortunately, information is more readily available than at any time in history. The Internet is leveling the playing field. Small companies can now compete against big companies. With a click of the mouse individuals can share ideas, gain insights, and communicate with people scattered around the globe. Information is being disseminated at rapid speeds on an unlimited number of topics. But knowledge alone, regardless of the medium, doesn't make us wise. It is what we choose to do with what we know that determines the life we dream to live. This is wisdom!

for Discussion

1. Write down the titles of your three favorite books.

2. Write down the titles of three books you intend to read, and determine when you plan to finish them.

3. Identify three people who could serve as mentors for you.

_____

_____

_____

_____

_____

_____

_____

_____

_____

_____

_____

_____

_____

_____

_____

_____

_____

_____

Chapter Six

△ *Wisdom—Your Knowledge in Action*

Since the beginning of time, philosophers have debated the origins of wisdom. Knowledge of complex subjects, such as the meaning of life and that which precedes it, the miraculous process of birth, has fueled the debates.

On the corporate, or even the street level, wisdom can mean two entirely different things, or just as likely, the same thing. CEOs define wisdom as one company's competitive advantage over an industry rival while retaining an enviable market share. "Street CEOs" view it from a survival-of-the-fittest perspective, where the strong rule the weak in the 'hood. Gangsta rap echoes this same inflammatory sentiment.

I've read many eloquent and thought-provoking definitions of wisdom through the years. But in its simplest form, wisdom is not only knowing what to do, but doing it right!

First, your vision must be secure. Faith activates the vision, and knowledge feeds it. Wisdom powers the engine for living the life you dare to live!

Again, you must be cognizant of the protective factors and risk factors before embarking on your journey. Why? Because wisdom needs some reference points to help guide you along.

Think of it this way. Today, cars are equipped with GPS interfaces to help drivers reach an intended destination. Wisdom is your GPS guide. It looks at where you are, and shows you how to arrive based on your protective factors.

Without these factors, your navigation system will be out of order! And please don't assume you know what they are. You must know them beforehand, or wisdom won't be of any use. Without foreknowledge, you run the risk of learning about these factors from your biggest, and most honest, critic (although not necessarily a bad thing).

"You're Cut!"

In the eighth grade I was cut for the first (and only) time from a 15-and-under AAU team coached by father-figure and disciplinarian, Nate Mitchell. The team was comprised of some of Columbus' most promising ninth graders, players such as Keith English and Tony Lucas. (Both Keith and Tony ended up playing college basketball at Division I schools.)

It never entered my mind that I would get cut from the team. If you've ever played team sports before, you know that being on the receiving end or seeing someone else get cut hurts to the core. Let me tell you, I was utterly devastated when Coach Mitchell called me in his office, which was adjacent to the basketball court at the Westside Boys and Girls Club, and gave me the news.

"You're cut!" he said. Not in a mean-spirited way, but he basically told me, "Look, your skill level doesn't warrant a spot on the team at this time. Besides, replacing an older player with equal talent and ability wouldn't be fair."

Some of my former teammates, happy that their name wasn't called, saw me leaving the building. They genuinely felt bad for me. Walking home distraught with my head hung down, I muttered, "Now, what do I do?"

> ## *"Never underestimate someone who has something to prove."*
>
> —Howard Bryant

Λ

But the period after I got cut was a time of introspection. I was inspired to develop a plan for overcoming skill-level deficiencies so that I could take my game to the next level. Prior to getting cut, I didn't take basketball very seriously since I played other sports. I worked on my game, but obviously, not enough.

Over the next several months, my practice time increased from one hour to four hours or more everyday. As a result, my game flourished the next year when I joined the AAU team that cut me when I was in the eighth grade. I even excelled above every player on that team and received higher rankings and greater recognition within the city, independent of grade. State and national honors soon followed. Getting cut was one of the best things to happen to me in my young basketball experience!

Here is a list of some of the world's most visible figures, past and present, who share a similar story. They were "cut down" but grew back stronger, which is what the seed of a setback should produce in our lives.

Failure List[3]

▲ Albert Einstein was four years old before he could speak.

▲ Isaac Newton did poorly in grade school and was considered "unpromising."

▲ Beethoven's music teacher once said, "As a composer, he is hopeless."

▲ When Thomas Edison was a youngster, his teacher told him he was too stupid to learn anything. He was counseled to go into a field where he might succeed by virtue of his pleasant personality.

▲ F.W. Woolworth got a job in a dry goods store when he was 21, but his employer would not permit him to wait on customers because he "didn't have enough sense to close a sale."

▲ Michael Jordan was cut from his high school basketball team. Boston Celtics Hall of Famer Bob Cousy suffered the same fate.

▲ A newspaper editor fired Walt Disney because he "lacked imagination and had no good ideas."

▲ Winston Churchill failed the sixth grade and had to repeat it because he did not complete the tests that were required for promotion.

▲ Babe Ruth struck out 1,300 times—a major league record.

▲ The Beatles were refused a contract and dismissed by Decca Records executives in 1962 who stated, "We don't like their sound. Groups of guitars are on the way out."

▲ After inventing the telephone, Alexander Graham Bell was told by President Rutherford B. Hayes, "That's an amazing invention, but who would ever want to use one of them?"

▲ R.H. Macy failed seven times before his store in New York caught on.

▲ Novelist John Creasey got 753 rejection slips before he published 564 books.

A setback can be the motivating factor we need to change the course of our destiny, forever. Leadership guru, John C. Maxwell, wrote in the book *Be a People Person*, "The Chinese symbol for crisis means danger. It also means opportunity. The key is to use a crisis as an opportunity for change."[4]

Wisdom recognizes eureka moments for what they are worth —opportunities to maximize talents, abilities, and financial resources that lie beneath the surface. The trauma I saw on the softball diamond as a young boy forced me to look at life from a different perspective than those who took part in the melee. Whether by choice or force, wisdom is necessary to open the door to achieving a life of greatness.

"It is not the strongest of the species that survive, nor the most intelligent, but the ones most responsive to change."

—Hereclitus

Λ

Setbacks or obstacles should redirect our focus. Our thoughts change. Our feelings change. Our actions change. Our priorities change. And our lives change for the better! Sometimes though, they can lead to our downfall when we see the glass half-empty instead of half-full.

Life's challenges compel us to change internally before we can become a change agent in the world. When we expect the world around us or our circumstance to change before we do, frustration and depression can take root in our lives, causing us to self-destruct. We complain. We pout. We eat more. We spend more. We stop praying. We lose faith and give up on life. Our lives spiral out-of-control and our goals, dreams, and visions, as well as talents and abilities, get buried in an overcrowded graveyard. Wisdom teaches us how to change and leads us to a productive future.

On The Same Page

When it comes to marriage, parenting, and personal finance, our nation's nuclear family faces formidable challenges like never before. Our assessment factors are again relevant to this discussion. An analysis of the factors in each of these categories follows.

For marriage, protective factors and risk factors (specific and in general) include:

Protective Factors	Risk Factors
faith in God, communication, mutual respect for one another's role, devotion to family, lifelong commitment, sacrificial love, quality mentors	family history of divorce, U.S. divorce rate, stumbling block of unforgiveness (for many married couples), physical attraction, busy schedules can hinder quality time

Today, the sanctity of marriage is threatened. Monya and I understand that marriage is a lifelong commitment. Sacrificial love between a husband and a wife create a bond so strong that nothing can tear it apart. Trust is another necessary ingredient that cultivates a healthy marriage.

> ### *"The strongest evidence of love is sacrifice."*
>
> —Caroline Fry

We got married in the midst of my NBA career. Friends and teammates asked, "Are you going to make Monya sign a prenuptial agreement since she'll be entitled to half of your assets if the two of you ever get divorced?"

I am not here to pass judgment on whether a wealthy husband-to-be should have his wife-to-be sign a prenuptial agreement, prenup for short. But from my point-of-view, prenuptial agreements breed distrust. If a wealthy man (or woman, for that matter) requests a prenup before getting married, then you wonder about their intentions. What message does this send to the other spouse? To the children?

When prenups are required, separate saving or checking or investment accounts are usually created. And the "what-if-we-get divorced?" cloud hangs in the air—over the spouses' and children's heads.

Our vision is to break the cycle of divorce in our family (as well as that of children born out of wedlock), leaving a legacy for Nyah and Lawrence Elijah and their children's children to emulate. But it starts with my wife and me. We don't want the word divorce to ever be a part of our vocabulary, or the kids! Yet, we do understand that divorce is the choice some couples, unfortunately, must make when abuse and/or infidelity breaks the chord of marriage and options to repair it have been exhausted.

To keep our marriage strong, we seek counsel from mentors (and sometimes total strangers!) who have successful marriages. We ask, "In one word, what is the secret to your unshakeable bond?"

"Flexibility."
"Patience."
"Compromise."
"Love."
"Trust."
"Honesty."

Our assessment factors also influence child-rearing. As parents, they can be:

Protective Factors	Risk Factors
sitting down at meals together, parental involvement at school, commitment to love, prayer, quality mentors, emotional support, family vision	short fuse when children are disobedient, parental abandonment (Lawrence), equitable distributions of time to each child, negative influences of child peer groups

In short, parenting is about giving and receiving love. At times, parenting requires tough love when children fail to respect parental authority!

In our minds eye, we see our children growing up to become adults who are balanced and complete spiritually, emotionally, relationally, physically, educationally, and financially. However, it is the seeds we plant (and the resulting choices they make) in their lives that determine, in large part, whether these goals come to fruition in adulthood.

> ### *"Love is the greatest advantage a parent can give."*
> —Warren Buffett
>
> Λ

I've often said that parenting is the world's greatest mentoring challenge. And gravitating to our protective factors increases the probability of positive outcomes in the lives of Nyah and Lawrence Elijah!

Every night before going to bed, I walk over to my daughter's room while she is sound asleep and kiss Nyah on her forehead and then whisper in her ear, "Daddy loves you." I know this resonates in her subconscious. As she reflects on the times we spend together, Nyah will grow up knowing how it feels when a man loves her. She will keenly understand the difference between male love and male lust.

> *"Perhaps once in a hundred years a person may be ruined by excessive praise, but surely once every minute someone dies inside for a lack of it."*
>
> —Cecil G. Osborne

A smooth talking wannabe player may try to get her attention by saying, "Let me love you the way you should be loved." Nyah's response will be apropros, "I've seen how my daddy treats my mom—the right way. And for as long as I can remember, he has given me the love that a daughter needs. So you got to come up with something newer than that tired line!" Ouch.

For Lawrence Elijah, when his piercing eyes connect with mine, looking deep into my soul, they tell me, "I expect you to be there and teach me how to be a good man when I grow up." Although an infant, the bond we share is intense. Also, his view of women, and subsequently, how he treats them, will be shaped by the actions that I display in this regard.

In my quest to become a great parent, I want to do everything that my father didn't. Attending play recitals, ball games, and church services with them. Supporting them educationally. And showering them with affectionate hugs that a father should gladly supply. Fathers greatly impact their child's identity, both male and female. He impacts them positively if he is committed to their well-being on a consistent basis. Negatively if he is non-existent. (Dr. Pamela A. Popper maintains that a protein in our upper respiratory system that protects us against colds, viruses, and other immune system attackers, is elevated for up to 48 hours when we are hugged by someone we care about!)[5]

Our assessment factors influence our ability to create wealth. The diagram at the top of the next page reflects some of the influences that may impact personal finance and investment decisions.

Protective Factors	Risk Factors
stewardship mentality, defensive asset allocation model (non-traditional diversification), live below means, regularly track expenditures, due diligence (raising financial IQ), charitable giving	unpredictable nature of investments, spousal differences over money fuel divorce in this country, future needs of aging parents, wealth transfer, ease of credit

Regardless of a family's income, personal finance often involves some painful tradeoffs. Half of all marriages in this country end in divorce. The usual culprit? Differences of opinion about money.

Marriage vows stipulate that "the two shall become one" and "til death do us part"; however, many couples add the disclaimer, "But not when it comes to money."

Privately, or in front of the kids, we don't argue about this traditionally taboo subject. But we agree that each expenditure should be scrutinized and documented (accompanied by a receipt or statement, which drives Monya crazy!).

No matter how insignificant the purchase, we keep track of them daily in a financial journal. (Please read **scouting your success** in Chapter Five if you need help setting up a realistic budget, or visit the website at www.thetriangleformula.com.)

Investment decisions are made jointly. We study trends and other economic data before making a move. Good friend and Merrill Lynch financial advisor, Daniel Levitt, has been a great resource, as well as other notable mentors.

Best-selling author of the *Rich Dad Poor Dad* series, Robert Kiyosaki, implores Americans to raise their financial IQ. With the looming Social Security crisis, corporate pension meltdowns, skyrocketing consumer debt, and household savings at historic lows (below 0 percent!), those who take advantage of financial knowledge will reap the rewards.

No longer can we depend on our employer to take care of us in retirement. That is a thing of the past, which makes it all the more important to manage our own financial futures.

"Learn then act" is the *Rich Dad Poor Dad* motto. The knowledge Monya and I have received and gleaned from mentors and personal assessments of economic trends have proved fruitful. Our asset allocation model is defensive in nature and has appreciated 30 percent or more in just about every investment class over the last several years. You don't need an MBA to become a successful investor, but a Ph.D. in due diligence is required for your specific situation!! (In certain instances, a certified investment specialist can assist you in your journey to achieve financial freedom.)

I will add that charitable commitments based on our heartfelt passions often open the door to unexpected financial and non-financial blessings. I encourage you to give at least 5-10 percent or more, if possible, of your income to an organization that is making a positive difference in our world.

The model we display when it comes to personal finance, investment decisions, and charitable giving may very well be imitated by our children. Whether taught or observed, they will at least glean something from the seeds we plant. When mom and dad handle money well, poorly, or with indifference—children usually follow suit.

Breakthroughs Come Through Setbacks

With every setback comes an opportunity. The key is to keep an open mind, a light heart, and a sense of optimism. Remember the vision you have for yourself and continue to seek knowledge and wisdom.

Perhaps you have recently been laid off from your job. You're already in debt and have crushing responsibilities to your children and your ailing parents. If you remain optimistic, continue networking and job-seeking, you might find an open window to opportunities greater than the door that was previously shut.

> *"Don't let the past*
> *contaminate the present."*
> —Dr. Keith Albow

Perhaps you just received news that you have been rejected from your dream college. You already had your future planned and had selected a course of study. The disappointment is even greater because all your friends got accepted. If you keep an open mind and consider other schools, you might find unexpected opportunities in an entirely new field of study, with a whole new set of friends!

Or perhaps you have been diagnosed with Type II diabetes. You don't want to spend the rest of your life taking shots of insulin, yet you know that this potentially debilitating disease requires medication. If you are willing to change your diet and exercise habits, you might be able to implement a plan that will reverse your diagnosis and result in a greater degree of health than you've ever had before.

Each of these setbacks represents an opportunity to transform an unfavorable situation into a favorable one. Whatever the setback, start gravitating to your protective factors. Your life will never be the same.

for Discussion

1. Name three people who have recovered from failure.

2. Name three times when you have benefited from failure.

3. Explain the meaning of this saying: "Failure needn't be fatal."

_____

_____

_____

_____

_____

_____

_____

_____

_____

_____

_____

_____

_____

_____

_____

Chapter Seven

The Spirit of Excellence

The spirit of excellence drives a poor student on an academic scholarship to bring his "A" game to a prestigious university. It compels a team of overachievers to reach for and win a championship. A new start-up company to squeeze into its place in a crowded industry. And a woman to bust through the glass ceiling as she attains a high-level management position.

I've studied the lives of successful athletes, parents, teachers, doctors, lawyers, CEOs, entrepreneurs, pastors, and rabbis, to hear what separates them from mainstream society. A sigh of relief overcomes me as they share the secret behind their extraordinary success. The spirit of excellence!

But are they somehow endowed with the trait of excellence by virtue of their race, economic class, or some other distinguishing factor?

> ### *"Excellence is to do a common thing in an uncommon way."*
>
> —Booker T. Washington

Λ

Contrary to the inclinations of some folk, excellence is not partial to any of these factors. However, it does demand that "club members" —regardless of their occupation or position—aspire to new heights of greatness each and every day. People who maintain the status quo are, by default, excluded from the club. And members who fall victim to the status quo mindset will have their memberships revoked immediately!

Excellence Membership Revoked

I am not ashamed to admit it, but I've had my membership revoked on several occasions. Boy was it costly!

Excellence has rules of engagement. When we fail to abide by those rules, we pay a heavy price. Spiritually. Emotionally. Mentally. Relationally. Socially. Physically. Financially. Educationally. We always lose something.

Not all of my choices have been wise. Chapter Eight of this book describes one of my most difficult lessons. I'll preview the lesson here by explaining that I got kicked off my high school team. My streak continued into college where my eventual departure from Indiana University cost me financially and publicly.

When you perform with excellence, you're less likely to be labeled. When you are negatively labeled, it is usually hard, though possible—to overcome. And when you are in the public eye, you are judged (rightly or wrongly) by what is reported in the media.

After my senior season of college, came the NBA draft. Teams still had questions about me, largely because of the tumultuous turn of events within a 12-month period, some five years earlier. Stepping back from excellence takes a tremendous toll.

Monetarily, I LOST tens of millions of dollars as a second round pick because I also failed to fully maximize my skills and abilities on the basketball court at Ohio State. I got caught up in college life and my press clippings. And I rarely worked on my game out of season; although adequate, I did just enough to get by. Big mistake. (Buckeye fans, please don't hold this public confession against me.)

"The quality of a person's life is in direct proportion to that person's commitment to excellence, regardless of the chosen field of endeavor."

—Vince Lombardi

Λ

The golden rule of excellence is that success is not a resting place; it is a journey. We must never be satisfied with where we are—the status quo mindset. When we underachieve, excellence rewards us what we're due—very little. Likewise, when we overachieve, excellence rewards us abundantly. Depending on our talents and our time limits, the window of opportunity for accomplishing our goals, dreams, or visions *contracts* slowly or quickly. Once it's closed, it is difficult, or nearly impossible to pry open. (Make no mistake. Businesses also suffer when they fail to take full advantage of their collective talents. Jim Collins' best-seller, *Good to Great*, illustrates the thin line between success and failure in the business world.)

Likewise, the window of opportunity to accomplish our goals, dreams, or visions *expands* slowly or quickly, depending, again, on our talent curve and time limit.

Unfortunately, when we squander our opportunities, excellence rewards the next person (or company) in line. This is particularly true in our 21st century global environment. Ever tried to register a domain name for your million dollar idea, only to find that someone else beat you to it while you were dragging your feet?

Now, why let the window of opportunity close and give your blessing away?

The Momentum Factor That Leads To Success

You may recall in earlier chapters my emphasis on the spirit of excellence as the hallmark of The Triangle Formula. One of the most popular financial magazines dedicated a bi-monthly edition to the subject of excellence. The edition was titled, *The Excellence Issue – What It Takes To Be Great*. Athletes, CEOs, politicians, musicians, and organizations were analyzed to determine how much of a factor excellence played in their success.

Greatness is achieved when we have something to shoot for, that is, vision. Faith to accomplish our vision comes next, followed by knowledge, wisdom, and excellence. And a goal, dream, or vision is never completed without its share of obstacles and setbacks.

In an organization, for-profit or non-profit, excellence starts at the top. Boeing CEO James McNerney told *Fortune* writer Geoffrey Colvin, "I have this idea in my mind. All of us get 15% better every year."[6] He initiates the goal; then he sets the tone for all employees to follow. James' quest for better results—every year—is what excellence is all about. Never satisfied with last year's, last quarter's, or even yesterday's success. If you want the life you dream to live, you don't have time for complacency, either.

As parents, if we want our kids to excel, we have to set the example when it comes to excellence in every area of our lives. Greatness can be duplicated through the DNA of the spirit of excellence.

Driven Through Paranoia

Excellence encompasses attributes such as hard work, discipline, determination, and yes, even paranoia. Let me explain. The season after my sophomore year, I met basketball guru Dan Downing. His insights helped take my game to the next level, especially this: "When you are not practicing to get better, someone else is."

For a time, Dan's comments created a state of paranoia within me. Practice was never the same again, because I didn't want my competition to catch up with me. Now my competition is global, and not just in the neighborhood.

"No plan is worth the paper it is printed on unless it starts you doing something."

—William H. Danforth

Λ

Three-time Super Bowl champion, quarterback Tom Brady of the New England Patriots, once stated that he always feels there's someone hunting him down on his footsteps. Healthy competition always brings out the best in vessels of excellence.

Imagine that you are the star runner on your track team. You've won every trophy since your freshman year. Now, you're a senior and expect to win a track scholarship to a major university. One afternoon, at track practice, you notice a new guy standing near the field. Your coach takes a moment to introduce him. Turns out, he's a transfer student, who's going to be running with your team, and he has always placed first. And during every practice run that day, he outruns you. What do you do? You have several options. Drop off the team. Sabotage your new adversary. Pout about all the bad breaks you get. Or rise to the occasion and accept the new competition as an opportunity to improve your already strong performance. With the right attitude, both of you can win. You might even break a few records.

Whether the contest is track, academics, or musicianship, we always meet competitors who have skills that we lack; but, again, healthy competition always brings out the best in vessels of excellence. Let the competition push you toward your best performance, ever.

On another note, poverty can have the same effect. When you've struggled, had to do without life's necessities, and have often gone to bed at night hungry, you can decide to change your mindset. A healthy mindset admits to starting at the bottom, while realizing you can only go up from "There."

MJ's Wake-up Call

If you've ever depended on a wake-up call to catch an important business meeting while staying the night in a hotel, you know the feeling. Sometimes we can get a wake-up call from an unexpected mentor to keep us focused on our journey. I got mine from Michael Jordan one evening on the basketball court.

It was 1997. After three seasons playing in Europe, I was finally in the NBA. I was a key reserve for the Sacramento Kings, and we were playing at home against the best team of the 1990's and one of the best teams of all-time—Michael Jordan's Chicago Bulls.

You remember Jordan. He was named to the All-NBA First Team 10 times, led the league in scoring 10 times, and won the NBA's Most Valuable Player award five times. Jordan led the Bulls to six NBA championships, and he became the standard by which every player thereafter would be measured. He was the best shooting guard to ever play the game—in fact, he was probably the best player ever at any position—and he was the ultimate competitor.

Of course, I was no slouch. I wasn't Michael Jordan, but for an NBA rookie, I was really "hooping" that year, really "doin' it," as they say on the streets. I only played about 20 minutes a game, but I was averaging almost 10 points and five rebounds. Projected over a normal 48-minute game, those numbers would've equaled 24 points and 12 rebounds per contest. Those were the kind of numbers normally produced every night by Tim Duncan, Karl Malone, and Kevin Garnett. In short, I was pretty impressed with myself.

I held my own against the All-Star big men in the league that year—Duncan, David Robinson, Garnett, Charles Barkley, Malone, and others. Before I came back from three years in Europe to play in the NBA, many people doubted I could even make the team, let alone make a contribution to the Kings. I was more than making a contribution—I quite often felt like "The Man."

That was the case on that particular night against the Bulls. The crowd was electric because Jordan, Scottie Pippen, and bad boy Dennis Rodman were in town. The city was in a buzz, and I was a part of the action.

To be honest, I was having a decent game—not a great one, but I was helping my team. That's not how I saw it at the time, though. At one point, I was fouled in the act of shooting, which sent me to the free-throw line for two shots. I started barking at anybody who would listen, especially Jordan and his legendary teammates. Never bashful about my talent and playing abilities, I said, "Nobody out here can stop me!"

Jordan heard me and was taken aback by my candor. "This ain't Ohio State, Lawrence," he said along with a few other words that I won't repeat. The greatest basketball player in the history of the game was putting me in my place. I was a brash kid trying to impress an icon of the game, and Jordan was telling me, "You haven't arrived yet!"

"Desire is the key to motivation, but it's the determination and commitment to unrelenting pursuit of your goal—a commitment to excellence—that will enable you to attain the success you seek."

—Mario Andretti

Δ

Talk about a smackdown . . .

Looking back, though, Jordan did me a favor. Sure, I'd overcome a lot of obstacles in my life to reach the pinnacle league of my sport, but I needed to keep everything in perspective. I beat the odds of growing up in Sullivant Gardens, a poverty- and crime-ridden housing project in Columbus, Ohio. I beat the odds of growing up without a father. I beat the odds while so many of my friends had failed to do so—they'd ended up hooked on drugs, dealing drugs, running with gangs, going to jail, and even dead.

I took advantage of the gifts God gave me—a height of 6-feet-9, the ability to play basketball, and, most importantly, a love of learning

—to escape the seemingly hopeless environment that trapped so many people. While my neighborhood peers fell around me, I won a state high school championship; played college basketball in the Big Ten for both Indiana University and The Ohio State University; was named All-Big Ten three years in a row; played professional basketball in Europe for three years; and then hooked up with the most elite basketball league in the world, the NBA.

After all those struggles, I was finally on the court with the greatest player in the game—and not just on the court with him, but talking trash to him. I definitely had overcome a lot, and my personal accomplishments seemed huge, but I would never have been there if not for other people in my life—mainly, the mentors.

"Don't [ever] be satisfied with where you are."

—Joel Osteen

Λ

Believe it or not, even Michael Jordan was a mentor for me in that moment. I call that being a mentor-in-passing. Jordan let me know that I still hadn't accomplished anything in the NBA except for getting there. To be successful, I couldn't rest on my laurels; I had to keep getting better. MJ was saying in effect, "Lawrence, you ain't done nothin' yet." I learned a lot in that one moment—mainly, that whatever your dream is, you have to pursue excellence every day to achieve it, even when you think you're already there. The spirit of excellence makes the difference between mediocrity and greatness. Excellence is a critical component of The Triangle Formula for success. Excellence reminds you to bring it every time. Your "A" game. Bring it. Every time.

On the court, on the job, in the classroom, on the page, on the stage. Whatever your endeavor, do it with excellence every time. Never give up on being excellent at what you do. You can't afford to let it slide one day this week just because you've been excellent for six days. Perseverance, overcoming adversity, and never, ever quitting, are all manifestations of an excellent spirit. Consistently excellent work, along with vision and faith, knowledge and wisdom, pave the road to success. I am committed to that road today, but for a short time in my life, I took a detour.

for Discussion

1. Name three benefits of achieving excellence in your pursuits.

2. Write down three personal qualities you wish to improve.

3. Name three people who are your biggest competitors; explain how competition is good for you.

_____

_____

_____

_____

_____

_____

_____

_____

_____

_____

_____

_____

_____

Chapter Eight

△ *Never, Never, Never, Never Quit*

1988 was a very good year. Statistically, I had just completed a stellar junior season at Wehrle High, averaging 28 points, 14 rebounds, 6 blocks, and 3 assists per contest. I was fortunate to be named Franklin County and State Player of the Year, and a consensus high school All-American.

Our team finished the season 26-2, garnering a USA Today Top 25 ranking as one of the nation's best teams. The two losses came in a national tournament hosted by Needham B. Broughton High School in Raleigh, North Carolina, alma mater of the legend, the late Pistol Pete Maravich. Pistol Pete died on January 5, 1988. I had the honor of meeting the legend a few weeks earlier at his alma mater, and he gave me some pointers on becoming a better shooter.

Naturally, I looked forward to my senior season and another state championship. But . . .

Six games into my senior campaign, Coach Chuck Kemper dismissed me from the team. The reason? Let's just say I needed an attitude adjustment, and Coach Kemper quickly noticed. Our once amicable relationship suddenly became strained as the recruiting sweepstakes for my talents grew more intense.

"If your popularity increases, don't be intoxicated by accolades."

△ —Deborah Smith Pegues

I was a top five prospect by then, being recruited by every bigtime college program in the country—North Carolina, Indiana, and UNLV, among many others—but my high school career was over. And I could kiss playing in the nationally televised McDonald's All-Star Game goodbye as well. Wehrle went on to win the state championship without me.

I exacerbated the problem by playing Russian roulette with my choice of colleges. Given the fortuitous turn of events, I felt the urge to commit and made a pact to sign with whichever coach called me first —North Carolina's Dean Smith or Indiana's Bobby Knight. It wasn't long before the call came. Coach Knight beat Coach Smith to the telephone after the news of my dismissal received national attention in USA Today and on ESPN. (Dean Smith has since retired as one of the game's greatest coaches. Coach Knight is now at Texas Tech with more wins than any other NCAA Division I college coach.)

Once my decision to attend Indiana University became public knowledge, all bets were on. Members of the media wagered that the marriage would never work. They were right. I didn't get booted off the team like I did in high school, but Coach Knight did kick me out of practice for lackluster play and told me to go home.

I went back to my apartment, packed my bags and took his advice, literally. I hit the road, unsure where I was going. Unbeknownst to me at the time, Coach Knight regularly applied this tactic to many players in Hoosierland, forcing them to focus on the task at hand. In retrospect, the dismissal was intended to humble me after my outstanding performance as a freshman. I had scored 26 points and was named to the Hoosier Classic all-tournament team.

My mother wasn't happy with my abrupt decision. Poignantly, she told me, "You've got to be a man, not a mouse. It's time to grow up even if you're only 19 years old."

In the span of exactly one year, my senior season of high school and freshman season of college went up in flames. Would I prove my growing list of critics right? Would I end up in basketball infamy like so many other basketball players from the streets of hard knocks who squandered their once-in-a-lifetime opportunity for basketball glory?

Have A Seat On The Bench

When I left Indiana, I enrolled at St. Catherine Junior College in St. Catherine, Kentucky. I never played there, but I enrolled during the second semester to continue my education. When the semester ended at St. Catherine, I returned to Indiana University. I went back to fulfill the obligation set by NCAA guidelines, which stipulated that I attend Indiana for one-year. Then I could transfer to the college of my choice.

I faced the onslaught of critics, but I never said anything negative about Bobby Knight or Indiana University. Bobby Knight was fair to me; he treated me with respect. He was a great coach, a genius. I take my share of the blame. I got kicked out of practice and it backfired.

The backlash from my choices might seem unfair, but it teaches an important lesson. The consequences of our actions can follow us for years. It is so important to weigh our choices and choose our actions carefully. What we do today can reverberate for a lifetime.

Sitting out, from 1989-1991, forced me to delay and analyze a secondary goal that didn't surface until my junior year of high school. This goal? A career in the NBA that few, very few, basketball players ever reach.

Due to NCAA guidelines, I had two years to reflect on my choices before getting the chance to play organized ball on the collegiate level again.

As I contemplated my future, NBA and college basketball analyst Bill Rafferty's epic words rang true. He said, "The best teacher you have is the bench."

Perhaps you've been sent to the bench as a result of corporate downsizing, a weight problem, a financial mishap, or any number of challenging setbacks. My advice to you is this. Don't quit. Prove your critics wrong; failure is not part of your DNA.

Motivator Les Brown once said, "Don't let someone's opinion of you become your reality." We must be candid about our mistakes (or those we are forced to bear), and then move on. If we get stuck in the quicksand of fear and self-defeat, our critics' dire predictions will regrettably come to pass.

The good news, for you and for me, is that life's challenges can be conquered. Again, we can conquer our challenges. That is, if we learn from them. You can start a thriving business. You can reach your desired weight. You can be financially free. You can graduate from high school and go to college. But will you stand tall and pass the test when difficulties come your way?

The Obstacle Course Of Life

Obstacles and tests have a purpose. They come to ignite or rekindle the fire to accomplish our dreams. Sometimes, these challenges remove the very thing stopping us from accomplishing our goals. It's our option to receive or reject their treasure trove of wisdom. Rick Warren, author of the best-selling book *The Purpose Driven Life*, wrote, "When you understand that life is a test, you realize that *nothing* is insignificant in your life. Even the smallest incident has significance for your character development."[7]

All obstacles have a purpose. A reason. An object lesson. A spiritual truth. They give us hope, faith, motivation, determination, courage, a forgiving spirit, compassion for others, integrity, loyalty, teamwork, and of course, wisdom.

"Problems are only opportunities in work clothes."

—Henry J. Kaiser

Consider these examples. Your grandmother is recovering from surgery. You visit her and try to comfort her in her pain, but she continually lashes out at you with angry words. Her anger is an obstacle to your once pleasant relationship and her words hurt your feelings. However, instead of lashing back at her or avoiding her altogether, you show her empathy and compassion. You speak the truth to her in love, sparing her feelings even though she has hurt yours. You also exhibit patience, looking forward to the day when she'll be back to her usual upbeat self. The way you respond to anger is the key. The correct responses—patience and the willingness to view life from another's perspective—build character.

Here's another example. You know you're good at your job, but you have a very competitive co-worker who enjoys showing you up. Your colleague is highly skilled, but needlessly arrogant, which creates an obstacle. You have a choice. You could undermine your co-worker's work ethic and damage his or her reputation. Or you develop your own skills and become an even stronger employee, knowing that others will eventually see and value your contribution to the organization.

Maybe you're a shy person and everyone in your circle of friends is an extrovert. Shyness can be an obstacle. However, you can overcome it in several ways. You can reach out to people and let them get to know you. Or you can recognize the value of being a different type of person, understanding that every person is designed for a purpose. The shy, sensitive, observant person might be just the one to meet the needs of another person who feels like an outcast.

Perhaps you fear speaking in public. You realize that your fear is an obstacle keeping you from achieving the success you visualize. Your choices are obvious. Either you avoid the limelight and remain mediocre in your pursuits, or you courageously exercise the willingness to fail on the way to becoming successful.

Obstacles such as these have tremendous value. A life without obstacles looks easy enough, but the pay-off is limited. When we rise to the challenge, we'll realize potential beyond our imagination.

Obstacles come for another reason—to remove a stronghold in our lives. A stronghold, such as fear, lack of faith, stubbornness, pride, arrogance, selfishness, greed, unethical behavior, complacency, indifference, resentment, anger, or an unforgiving heart, stops us from moving forward and accomplishing a life of greatness. Likewise obstacles can come to remove a person from our lives. When someone is hindering our development, we might notice how obligations and schedule conflicts create obstacles that hamper the relationship.

> ## *"If people don't add to your life, they'll surely take from it."*
>
> —Emmanuel Judkins

Δ

Sometimes, we repeat the same self-defeating pattern for years, and not learning from our mistakes. At other times, the lessons take different forms. Either way, object lessons repeat themselves until we willingly let go of these burdens.

A successful businessman breaks free of the greed disease and gives 20 percent of his profits to the poor. Almost overnight, his business flourishes as he pledges and makes good on his promise to give even more wealth away.

A young father releases the misdeeds of his father in childhood, which allows him to love his two children as every parent should.

A resentful mother stops criticizing her daughter after she overhears her daughter repeating the same bitter words to her younger siblings.

A single woman overcomes her indifference and adopts several children when she sees fulfillment in the homes of people giving foster care.

Obstacles pull us, stretch us, shape us, and mold us so that we can navigate through the course of life. We can't choose where we start, but we can keep to the direction set before us by our protective factors.

Bring On The Chitlins!

Tyler Perry (of Madea fame) is an African American icon in the urban theatre and stage show circuit. His movies and plays, too numerous to mention, have grossed several hundred million dollars in less than a decade. And they're still growing when you count DVD sales!

A man who wears many hats, the actor-producer-director-comedian-businessman-psychologist (well, he does inspire loyal followers to persevere in the midst of difficulties through humor!) continues to add to his vast fortune and legacy. Tyler signed a contract with TBS to produce a sitcom that could—get this—air five nights per week. Industry critics rolled their eyes when they heard about the possible $200 million dollar deal, fuming, "He is out of his league in the prime time, ultra-competitive network venue." Time will tell whether this venture pans out for Tyler.

The brother even has a small crowd of detractors within his own camp of all places—the African American community. Traditionalists view his chitlin circuit act as self-deprecating, claiming the shows cast a bad light on blacks due to the stereotypical portraits of ghetto life. A grandmother named Madea carries a pistol in her purse and isn't bashful when it comes to starting (and ending) a family or neighborhood feud. Black men run around like dogs in heat and fail to take responsibility for their children born out of wedlock. His humor can, admittedly, cause some audience members not familiar with 'hood heartache to squirm in their seats. But in spite of his shock-and-jolt message, Tyler always ends every story with a ray of hope: tomorrow can be better than today.

He should know.

Tyler grew up poor in New Orleans. His family of six lived in a cramped house, the type which, unfortunately, is all too familiar to us since witnessing the Third World atmosphere of poverty, despair, and hopelessness of invisible, forgotten New Orleanians caught in the wake of Hurricane Katrina.

In an interview with *Fortune* magazine writer Nadira A. Hira, Perry shared an interesting phenomenon common in downtrodden communities. "Where I come from, you can have your dream, but keep it private. Don't share it with anybody, because they'll try to take it from you and snuff it out."[8] Tyler mentioned that "he attempted suicide twice" while battling the demons of depression.

He moved to Atlanta in his early twenties to birth his dream. Tyler's first stage play failed miserably, losing every penny he'd saved —$12,000. He created show after show and worked job after job to finance his dream. All of his stage plays ended in failure. By then, he was finally ready to close the curtain and call it quits. That is, until by trial-and-error Tyler discovered his jackpot audience—working class church folks who weren't afraid to support his brand of humor.

"You have to deal with failure; then you have to keep performing and performing."

—Rudy Giuliani

One hit stage show turned into several hundred per year, with audience members totaling tens of thousands per week. More importantly, the underlying theme behind Tyler's unconventional theatre and movie success is this: never, ever give up in the face of adversity.

Obstacles and bench-warming sessions come to test us to see if we are worthy of the goals, dreams, and visions that have been deposited into us from above.

We might be surprised at where these dreams lead us and who our lives touch. We are blessed when we live according to these principles for success, and beyond our own success, we become blessings to other people who reap the benefits of our vision, knowledge, and excellence.

for Discussion

▽

1. Name three times when you've faced an obstacle in your life.

2. How did you overcome those obstacles?

3. Why is it a good thing to face obstacles?

_____

_____

_____

_____

_____

_____

_____

_____

_____

_____

_____

_____

_____

_____

_____

_____

Chapter Nine

The Lawrence Funderburke
△ Youth Organization

While working as a vendor at Cooper Stadium, I made a promise to God:

> "Lord if you ever place me in a prominent and influential position when I get older, I promise to give back and help others. I promise."

The seed was planted more than two decades earlier at the age of 12 to help youth from backgrounds similar to mine. When you're dealing with kids, your life has to be in order in order to get theirs in order. I had attained success in my line of work as an NBA basketball player, but I needed to answer an important question: What is the best way to make an impact on young people?

In 2000, the **Lawrence Funderburke Youth Organization** (LFYO) was established to improve the lives of disadvantaged youth through financial literacy and economic empowerment, career role modeling, and educational field trips. LFYO has operated in Sacramento, California, and Columbus, Ohio. (For more information on LFYO, please visit www.LFYO.org.)

Our three-tier approach gives needy youngsters hope for a better tomorrow. Some people have asked, "Why bother teaching financial literacy to economically challenged young people and communities?" For me, the answer lies within my own life.

Before transferring to Wehrle High, I attended Worthington Christian High School as a freshman and sophomore. Located in the Worthington suburb of Columbus, the school was a little more than a half an hour drive from my neighborhood, although it seemed like I was leaving for another planet.

Being one of only a handful of blacks didn't bother me, nor did the challenging curriculum. But the economic gap between the other "rich" students and me was difficult to overcome. An innocent comment by my coach's son, then five-year old Jason Weakley, really opened my eyes to the wealth gap that still exists in our world today.

Coach Scott Weakley and his family would often pick me up to eat dinner with them. One day, as I got in the car, young Jason caught me (and everyone else) off guard. Observing the scenery of Sullivant Gardens—very little grass and lots of trash—and having difficulty saying my first name, he asked, "Hey Warrence. Hey Warrence. Are you poor?"

"The harvest of our future
depends on the seeds
that we plant today."

—Howard Tillman

Λ

His father, mother, and two brothers were as shocked as I was. So shocked that no one knew what to say next. As the tension melted, I responded, "Let's just say our family doesn't have a lot of money." During the rest of the ride to the Weakley home, hardly anyone said a word, reflecting instead on the shocking words of a very observant little boy.

"War"rence: At War On Poverty

Poverty made me feel uncomfortable, as it did young Jason that day. It even compelled him to inquire about my economic situation and living environment.

When you're poor, some people consider you invisible, just taking up space in an overcrowded world. Even if they never say what they're thinking, their vibe says it all.

The Lawrence Funderburke Youth Organization is at war with poverty, much like iconic rock singer Bono and his ONE Campaign, which aims to make poverty history. LFYO has a domestic reach that teaches compassionate capitalism, which I discussed, in addition to the importance of leadership, with former New York City Mayor Rudy Giuliani over lunch one day at the New Albany Country Club. At the very least, the poverty mindset must be eradicated from our nation of boundless opportunities.

Critics, those who see the glass as half-empty, argue that eliminating poverty is an unrealistic goal. Unfortunately, too many youth from poor backgrounds view their current situation and future through the same prism.

"Literally, the future of our country is at stake."

—Oprah Winfrey

Δ

Renowned pastor T.D. Jakes stated, "Something familiar can be fatal because you see yourself as being what you went through, rather than understanding that you can go through it and not be it." That is why we expose youth to the opposite of poverty to expand their vision of the world in which we live.

ROM – Return On Message

I often get invited to speak to young people. I am as focused and intense with them as I was in any basketball game I played. I realize the awesome privilege in front of me: to communicate a message that resonates down to their core. I usually have one shot to leave an indelible mark that has the potential to last a lifetime!

One morning I met with students at West Broad Street Elementary school in Columbus' Hilltop community, which has been the forgotten feature of the city's makeover. Development dollars have not made their way there. It pretty much looks the same as it did 20 years ago when I was a child.

The morning I visited West Broad Elementary, Kamal Ansari, the principal, made an unexpected request. He asked me to share a motivating message with his students. I obliged and discussed the Triangle Formula of Success. Stories pertaining to vision and the spirit of excellence kept their attention. But when I emphasized the relevance of school, particularly knowledge, I had a surprise for them. To their astonishment, I gave them the opportunity to win some big money. Now they were really interested! (Okay, $120 today isn't what it used to be.) Right on cue during the middle part of my speech I asked several trivia questions. (Sorry, I can't tell which questions I ask, but I'll give you a hint: They usually have to do with money!!)

In the first class I visited, one knowledgeable eight-year old boy answered the $50 trivia question correctly. I was surprised since many adults do not know the answer. After I'd finished speaking with a second group of students, their teacher, Nancy Moore, stopped me in the hallway and said, "Twenty minutes after you left, the entire class was still talking about vision, knowledge, and excellence—The Triangle Formula of Success!"

In the second class I visited, one student won $20.

During my final class of the day, I addressed a bright young lady who, once again, got the $50 question correct.

The lesson to students at the conclusion of my speech is always the same: "You always make money with knowledge. The more knowledge you have—and it starts with school—the more money you'll make as an adult!"

In the business world, financial advisors and investors analyze an investment by the return it generates, or ROI—return on investment. I would gladly invest $120 in these kids because I know my ROM—the return on my message—will compound with interest in their lives.

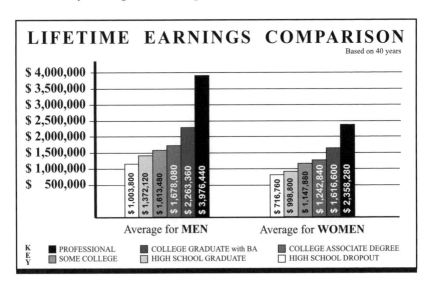

LIFETIME EARNINGS COMPARISON

Based on 40 years

Average for **MEN** — Average for **WOMEN**

Men: $1,003,800 / $1,372,120 / $1,613,480 / $1,678,080 / $2,263,360 / $3,976,440

Women: $716,760 / $998,800 / $1,147,880 / $1,242,840 / $1,616,600 / $2,358,280

KEY: PROFESSIONAL · COLLEGE GRADUATE with BA · COLLEGE ASSOCIATE DEGREE · SOME COLLEGE · HIGH SCHOOL GRADUATE · HIGH SCHOOL DROPOUT

Compassionate Capitalism At A Glance

Let's consider our current situation in America. The future of our great democracy is at stake. Across the nation, 30 percent (and probably higher) of incoming high school freshmen fail to stay the course and graduate. The repercussions are staggering.

In LFYO's financial literacy Power Point Presentation, we address the Million Dollar Mistake, as reflected in the diagram on the previous page. Young people who fail to graduate from high school will make one million dollars less over the course of their lifetime than peers who go on to college and earn a meaningful degree. The difference doubles, or in some cases triples, with graduate or professional degrees, such as an MBA, law degree, or Ph. D.

According to the most recent statistics, the number of high school dropouts is estimated at "about 1.3 million students nationwide."[9] They are frustrated with their learning curve. They are bored and unmotivated to stay the course and graduate from high school. In fact, the likelihood that many of them will be incarcerated and live in poverty as adults is likewise problematic.

"We are losing our kids because we haven't built relationships with them."

—Josh McDowell

Δ

Here is why keeping at-risk youth focused on education is so vitally important.

Dr. William Bainbridge, a distinguished research professor and regular contributor to the *Columbus Dispatch*, the *Florida Times-Union*, and EducationNews.org, shared some alarming statistics on this epidemic. High school dropouts:

- ▲ Contribute disproportionately to the unemployment rate. Fifty-five percent of young adult dropouts are employed, compared with 74 percent of high-school graduates.
- ▲ Pay about 50 percent less than what graduates pay in state and federal taxes. Over a working lifetime, that amounts to about $60,000 per dropout.
- ▲ Constitute 75 percent of state prison inmates and 59 percent of federal inmates and are 3.5 times more likely than graduates to be incarcerated.

Impact Of High School Dropouts (U.S. Department of Education)[10]

Dr. Bainbridge noted also, "For those who fail to graduate from high school, the economic lessons are enormous. Over the course of a lifetime, the gap in earning potential between a high school dropout and a high school graduate is $260,000."[11] Unrealized tax receipts and lost productivity, and squandered purchasing power can exceed well over $300 billion as a result of a million youth who drop out of high school. Obviously this discrepancy could affect the urban and suburban dweller alike. The burden on government spending for social programs would rise substantially, as well. According to the Center for American Progress, "The United States' global competitiveness and the economic self-sufficiency of our citizens are at stake."[12] Perhaps this knowledge will motivate us even further to help at-risk youth.

> ### *"The language our kids are exposed to often dictate how those kids will perform in school."*
> —Geoffrey Canada

Let us assume that 50 percent of youth who participate in our program are at risk of not graduating from high school. What would be the financial impact to the country if they go on to graduate? In the span of five years where we would cater to 1,000 participants, and if we were successful in assisting one-half of them in just their efforts to graduate high school, they would earn roughly $13,000,000 more over the course of their lifetimes than if they had dropped out. At a marginal tax rate of 25 percent, our government would realize $3,250,000 in tax receipts. If all of them graduate from both high school and college, this would create $500 million in additional wealth, tax receipts ($125,000,000 compared to $3,250,000), and productivity, which is the unknown factor since it is difficult to analyze hypothetically. But it would be likewise significant.

LFYO embraces the same pillars of success—vision, knowledge, and excellence—as the Triangle Formula. We help participants cultivate the vision for their future through career role models and educational field trips.

LFYO presents doctors, lawyers, financial advisors, realtors, dentists, and a host of other realistic professionals who offer career advice and mentoring support to the students. Notice that professional sports and the entertainment field are not mentioned, since these occupations are, for the most part, unrealistic for the average person.

Perhaps the most effective method to help develop long-term thinking occurs when we take them to places they've never been before. Every year LFYO arranges field trips to five-star restaurants, such as Ruth's Chris Steak House in Columbus and The Firehouse Restaurant in Sacramento. Participants who qualify are escorted in limousines and given a lesson in fine-dining etiquette.

"Sometimes in order to help people you have to take them out of their environment."

—T.D. Jakes

Faces light up as excitement builds. On this day, they feel very special. Most of them reference the moment in the context of being a celebrity. Students reflected on the experience in letters addressed to LFYO. Two of the letters especially stood out:

> "Thank you for the field trip. It was fun and I loved the limousine. I am glad that the food was delicious. Why do you have this program? I think I know. It's because you love teaching. We appreciate it."
>
> —Jennifer C.

> "Thank you for the food at the really nice restaurant. I liked the ice cream a lot. I learned how to use two forks. It was fun riding in the limousine, and I liked being dropped off at home in it. This program is helping me. We thank you so much for being here for us."
>
> —Kyle C.

The experience is surreal, but I give them a simple lesson to take-away with them. "Continue doing the right things and a life of modest luxury can be yours in adulthood. Look around. There are no celebrity patrons, just successful doctors, lawyers, businesswomen, and entreprepreneurs here!" We've also taken students to financial institutions to show how wealth is managed, as well as television studios, museums, and college campuses, to name just a few.

In Sacramento, one student named Ulma mentioned to my wife as the limousine pulled up to her home to drop her off, "I don't ever want this day to end." Moments like this, we'll never forget, either.

These unique field trips build students' vision and knowledge base and provide career advice and insights. Our youth-friendly Power Point presentations cover topics such as financial planning, budgeting, credit management, risk management, career assessment, savings and investments, insurance, and portfolio analysis, and many other topics related to financial literacy. (We teamed up with MidState Educators Credit Union to develop the *Money Keepin' It Real!* Program.)

In Reality Day exercises, students start to develop an appreciation for the difficult financial choices that adults regularly face. Reality Day consists of trial-and-error exercises. Each participant practices making personal financial choices, while learning how to achieve and maintain a desirable lifestyle as a functioning adult. The pay they receive from their assigned occupation is directly correlated to random grade point averages and attendance records. A contest featuring financial literacy expert, Robert Kiyosaki's *Cashflow for Kids* board game allows participants to win additional monies for their accounts. The game addresses the importance of passive income, portfolio management, and debt reduction.

"It's independent self-sufficiency that eliminates poverty."
Λ   —John Gregory

We see it as imperative that we plant a financial seed into their lives to start them on the path to financial freedom. Each participant who completes the program is awarded a $100 Certificate of Deposit. (For the 2009 school year, the Ohio Senate recently passed a bill making it mandatory for financial literacy to be taught in high schools as part of the social studies curriculum.)

All of these components drive home the point that school will be critically important to their financial well-being as adults, especially with household savings levels at historic lows, skyrocketing consumer debt, corporate pension meltdowns, and the looming social security crisis. Today's youth must raise their financial IQ in order to deal effectively with these issues in adulthood. (Some students have even helped their parents in this area!)

Two past members received college scholarships in the 2007-2008 school year. Joe Smith has been accepted at Miami University, a prestigious private school in Ohio, and Joseph Easley will attend Ohio Dominican University in Columbus. Smith wrote in a letter:

> "I am so glad that you volunteered your useful information to help guide us to a successful life and career. I would have never imagined that managing money could be such a big issue. You see, if I had all that money that big stars had, I would most likely blow it, too. By using the financial information you presented, I can be a successful 'money manager.' You can only give us the ball; it's up to us to make the shot."

Lastly, excellence is about practicing what we preach to the kids—education, respect and compassion for others, and keeping our word. I am a proponent of higher education, having graduated with a degree in Business Finance (magna cum laude) and a master's in Business Administration.

The most valuable asset we have is time, which involves helping others less fortunate. Children hold staff to the promises we make in and out of the classroom. The goal is to always deliver, because we are only as credible as our track record. (Besides, children are like elephants. They never forget anything when it comes to a promise. Am I right, parents?)

The Legacy We Leave Behind

While a vendor during my teenage years, selling popcorn and peanuts and cracker jacks, I had to walk back and forth every day past a graveyard, which was sandwiched between Sullivant Gardens and Cooper Stadium. And I often thought to myself, "Who were those people while they spent their brief time here on earth? What did they do? Where did they live?" Today I'd like to know, "What legacy did they leave behind?"

How do I want to be truly remembered? For the number of points that I scored? By my press clippings? The amount of money in my bank account? By material success? No, I want to be remembered for the number of lives I helped to change and transform for the better, starting with my family! That is what I want engraved on my tombstone.

Former OSU football star and NFL player, Todd Bell, died of a sudden heart attack at the tender age of 47 in 2005. But before he passed, Todd laid the groundwork to improve retention and graduation rates for OSU African American male students. The Black Male Initiative, in conjunction with the Office of Minority Affairs and the Office of Student Affairs, was born in 2002.

Todd's leadership has given African American males, young men with a vision for their futures, the necessary resources in the form of mentors and academic support staff to graduate. Upon hearing the news of his untimely passing, the resource center changed its name to commemorate his efforts. In the heart of Ohio State's campus, the Todd Anthony Bell National Resource Center on the African American Male resides.

Daphne Bell, Todd's widow, said, "Football was the avenue to get my husband to his purpose." During his career, Todd was one of the most feared hitters in the game. Never one to bask in the spotlight, though, his message of hitting the books as a vital key to success resonated with the young men he touched even to this day. One of his many protégés, Yavez Ellis, said at a fundraiser honoring the memory of Todd Bell, "Success is not a color; it is a characteristic." A college or technical education gives our young people a legitimate chance to succeed in life. Todd's legacy embodies this belief.

"We can worry more about helping the world to the extent that we can worry less about helping ourselves."

—Geoff Colvin

Λ

The following story highlights the necessity to reach out to at-risk youth full of promise and unlimited potential, although some people tend to write them off as hopeless misfits to society-at-large. In an email, Sidney Baker agreed to share his story, typical of many of our nation's inner-city males. I had the pleasure of meeting him over the Christmas Holiday at his uncle's house in Tampa, Florida:

> "I grew up in public housing in Atlanta, Georgia. For more than a month after my birth, the doctor proclaimed that it was exceedingly improbable for a premature baby living with the support of a breathing machine to survive. My mother has always been absent in my life, going in and out of jail,

because of her drug addiction. I have never seen my father, nor do I know who he is. However, my loving great-grand-mother raised and provided for me the best she could. I am so thankful for her because she instilled in me the values of determination, tolerance, and intelligence as essential ingredients of success. Although we could not afford expensive toys and clothes, my grandma provided all the love and care I needed.

"My goal is to leave the world a much better place than when I found it."

—Dwayne Wade

Λ

"Since kindergarten, I have always liked and excelled at school. I saw school as competition; I always worked hard to get the best grades I possibly could. While growing up, my competitive nature led me to develop a love for playing sports. I played a sport every season, including baseball, basketball, and football. Instead of having nothing to do and getting in trouble after school, I was at practice. I attribute sports—one of my protective factors—for keeping me involved in something I love and out of all the trouble that was easy to find in my community.

"People such as my uncle and other significant people that I have met throughout my life introduced me to another world outside of my community. They showed me that there is a better life waiting to be achieved if I am willing to work hard for it. For as long as I can remember, my uncle has always been a positive role model and mentor in my life.

"I have realized that this world is full of opportunities, regardless of your color, sex, creed, or culture. The condescending view of society towards African Americans is what lit the fire that opened my eyes to the world of plentiful opportunities. I only yearn that more African Americans would aim to prove society wrong.

"My ultimate goal is to become a distinguished businessman who possesses a wholesome family, great health, and financial stability. I hope to inspire others whom society has written off. I plan to earn a degree in Finance and Economics from Georgetown University. Also, I am in search of a summer internship in Finance/ Investment Banking, so I would like it if you could help me with this request!"

You never know how much of an influence you can be in the life of an impressionable young person. The opportunity to make a lasting difference has never been greater than it is today.

"You cannot live a perfect day without doing something for someone who will never be able to repay you."

—John Wooden

Δ

for Discussion

1. What are some of the needs in your community?

2. Write down three causes that you want to work toward.

3. Use the following pages to document how you will use *The Triangle Formula of Success* in your life and work.

_____

_____

_____

_____

_____

_____

_____

_____

_____

_____

_____

_____

_____

_____

_____

∇

Closing Remarks

"Die empty"

The following story was told to me recently by a college professor:

> *"An old gentleman, a very wise man from Africa, who I would
> see year-after-year in my travels there, would often tell me,
> 'Die empty. Die empty.'*
> *One time I had a chance to pull him aside and I asked,*
> *'Please elaborate. What do you mean by die empty?'*
> *He said, 'The richest place on earth is not the diamond or gold
> mines here in Africa. The richest place on earth is the cemetery,
> because there lies the hopes and dreams of men and women.*
> *Songs that have never been sung.*
> *Books that have never been written.*
> *So your goal is to die empty.*
> *Everything that the Creator has put in you—talents, abilities,
> and skills—He wants in you so that it is given out and left
> for the benefit of others here on planet earth.*
> *Everything that's in you, you want to give out.*
> *So that at the end of your journey, you can
> die empty.'"*

I wish you all the best in your journey down the road of success. May all of your goals, dreams, and visions be accomplished through The Triangle Formula for the benefit of our world.

Would love to hear from you.
Please email your story to: **Lawrence@TheTriangleFormula.com**

Warmest regards,

Lawrence Funderburke

About the Author

Lawrence Funderburke

As Founder and Executive Director of the **Lawrence Funderburke Youth Organization** (LFYO), Lawrence oversees operations that assist at-risk youth through financial literacy and economic empowerment, career role models, and educational field trips (www.LFYO.org). A prolific writer and motivator, he is the author of *Hook Me Up, Playa!*, a book that examines the financial trials and tribulations of modern-day professional athletes.

On behalf of LFYO, Lawrence has received numerous awards and recognitions for his devotion to the community, including the first-ever NBA's Hometown Hero of the Month Award and the National Silver Medallion Award by the Boys and Girls Clubs of America for outstanding service to youth through the Boys and Girls Club movement. LFYO has also been recognized by the Sacramento City Council and Mayor Michael Coleman of Columbus for service to the community.

The All Big-Ten performer played basketball at The Ohio State University from 1992-1994, and received his Bachelor of Science degree in Business Finance (magna cum laude) in 1994. In 2006, he completed an executive education program at Stanford University, covering risk assessment of various investment tools and other business-related topics. In June of 2007, Lawrence completed his MBA from the University of Phoenix as well as an executive education program on value investing at Columbia University.

A native of Columbus, Ohio, Lawrence played professional basketball for eleven years from 1994-2005, with eight in the NBA and three overseas. He and his wife Monya have two children, Lawrence Elijah and Nyah.

Glossary and End Notes

Unless otherwise indicated, definitions adapted from: Dictionary.com Unabridged (v 1.1). Random House, Inc. 10 Jul. 2007. Dictionary.com http:// dictionary.reference.com.

Apropos – Fitting; at the right time; to the purpose, opportunely; opportune; pertinent: apropos remarks.

Asset Allocation Models – Asset allocation models can be used as a guide when choosing investments and are commonly found in retirement plans. These models are designed to reflect the personal goals and risk tolerance of the investor. (Definition from americanfundsretirement.retire.americanfunds.com.)

Due diligence – The process of evaluating the risks and rewards of a personal, financial, or professional investment. A way of preventing unnecessary harm to either party involved in a transaction.

Status quo – The existing order of things; present customs, practices, and power relations: "People with money are often content with the status quo." From Latin, meaning "the state in which."

Toxicology screen – These are various tests to evaluate the type and approximate measurement of legal and illegal drugs in a person's system. (Definition provided by Rydell Gibson.)

END NOTES

[1] Myles Munroe, The Principle and Power of Vision (New Kensington, 2003) 223.

[2] Akrit Jaswal Interview, January 12, 2007, "The Oprah Winfrey Show."

[3] Anonymous, Failure List of The Famous, http://www.inspire21.com/site/stories/ failurelist.html.

[4] John C. Maxwell, Be a People Person (Colorado Springs, 1989) 61.

[5] Pamela A. Popper, Wellness 101: The Complete Health and Wellness Course, PB Industries, Inc., Worthington, OH, 2005.

[6] Geoffrey Colvin, "How One CEO Learned to Fly," Fortune, October, 2006.

[7] Rick Warren, The Purpose Driven Life, (Grand Rapids, 2002) 45.

[8] Nadira A. Hira, Diary of a Mad Businessman, http://money.cnn.com/magazines/ fortune/fortune_archive/2007/02/19/8400222/index.htm.

[9] Sarah Holt, High School Dropouts Cost the U.S. Billions in Lost Wages and Taxes, According to Alliance for Excellent Education, http://www.all4ed.org/pres/ pr_022806.html.

[10] William Bainbridge, High School Dropouts Cost Nation Billions in Lost Wages and Taxes, http://www.schoolmatch.com/articles/ftu2006Apr15.cfm.

[11] Ibid.

[12] Adria Steinberg, Cassius Johnson, and Hilary Pennington, Addressing America's Dropout Challenge, http://www.americanprogress.org/issues/2006/11/graduation.html.

The Triangle Formula of Success

KNOWLEDGE

EXCELLENCE

VISION